THE SAGA OF A CORNISH FAMILY
1882-1975

The Saga of a Cornish Family 1882-1975

Elizabeth Flawn

UNITED WRITERS
Cornwall

UNITED WRITERS PUBLICATIONS LTD
Ailsa, Castle Gate, Penzance, Cornwall.

British Library Cataloguing in Publication Data:
A catalogue record for this book is available from the British Library.

ISBN 1 85200 062 7

Printed in Great Britain by
United Writers Publications Ltd
Cornwall

To my parents
Claude and Muriel Sara
in loving memory.

CONTENTS

		Page
	Introduction	9
1	Early Beginnings	11
2	A Granddaughter's Memory of her Grandparents Elizabeth and Charles Tyack	20
3	The Sara Family	25
4	Courtship and Marriage	29
5	Separation	36
6	Tasmania	40
7	Egypt	48
8	Russia	54
9	Journey Home	65
10	Wartime in Britain, 1915-1918	75
11	Mabel and Harry Tyack	80
12	Peace	88
13	Trinidad	94
14	Thorneloe	109
15	1923	113
16	Venezuela	119
17	Looe	125
18	St. Dennis	134
19	The Second World War	143
20	St. Newlyn East	153
21	Adieu	156

INTRODUCTION

This is a true story, the story of my parents Claude and Muriel Sara and their families, spanning the years between the late nineteenth century and 1975.

It is essentially a love story, a story of loyalty and endurance, but also of travel and adventure.

My father, as a geologist and surveyor, travelled widely. The book includes life on the gold fields of Tasmania, the Egyptian desert, the oil fields of Russia and the family's escape from Russia in 1915. It continues with their years spent in the West Indies, the visit of Edward, Prince of Wales, to Trinidad and an expedition to Venezuela.

They say that Cornishmen travel the world but come home to roost, and my father was no exception. In his forties he became ordained as a priest in the Church of England and the latter part of this book relates to life in Cornwall as a parson.

The book also includes experiences in the First and Second World Wars and the London Blitz.

The material in the early part of the book is obtained from hundreds of letters my parents wrote to one another and to their children which I have inherited, and also from written accounts left by my mother and stories told to me in childhood. The latter part is written from personal memory.

I am greatly indebted and sincerely grateful to Mrs Shirley Bazett for her most generous and untiring help in planning and typing the whole of the final draft of this book, without whose help this work would never have been completed.

I would also like to express my thanks to Mrs Mary Noall, Mrs Mira Little and Mrs Rita Griffith.

A special thanks to. Stanley B. Hough for his encouragement, criticism and advice, and also to my husband for reading proofs, his patience and long suffering. He died suddenly on 3rd November 1992.

1

EARLY BEGINNINGS

Muriel was brought up in the Cornish mining town of Camborne. Theirs was a business house, a bustling, busy house, with lots of comings and goings. Behind the business lay the kitchen with its Cornish range, scrubbed table and tiled floor which was well sanded. Behind the kitchen was the large scullery with a copper for boiling up the family clothes. The breakfast-room was also on the ground floor. On the first floor lay the dining-room, with its rich mahogany furniture. A service lift connected it with the kitchen below. There was also a schoolroom opening on to a flat roof. In front, the sunny bay-windowed drawing-room looked out on the church and the busy street below. Five bedrooms occupied the top floor, three with bay windows looking out on to the street - the girls' room, parents' room and spare room. Sometimes the spare room was occupied by a governess, Miss Sidebottom or Miss Botterell. Grandma slept in the back bedroom with a view over the countryside, and at the end of a long passage the boys had a large bedroom. The best view, and the most popular, was from the upstairs landing window.

Muriel, a long-legged girl, loved to sit on the landing window-seat, looking across the rolling countryside to the sea, the Atlantic ocean. There was nothing between it and America. To the mining community of Cornwall, America seemed less far away and strange than London. Cornish miners travelled the world but came home to roost, with all their strange tales of foreign parts. The landing window was a favourite place, especially in the evenings when the golden ball of the sun was sinking into the sea and the sky was a glory of red and gold.

Muriel was a thin girl with an expressive animated face. She had dark luminous eyes and dark hair tied in a bow at the back. It was her proud boast that she could sit on her hair, and her beloved eldest brother Harry was proud of it too, and took great pleasure in brushing it as they sat by the fire in the evenings. Muriel had the beautiful colouring, bright cheeks and translucent look which so often go with tuberculosis. She had a vivacious personality; in after years, someone describing her to me said: "She was like a flash of light." Another said, "She was the prettiest woman I ever saw." There was something fey about Muriel. Her sister Mabel, the practical one, would say scornfully: "Muriel and her nonsense."

On Saturdays their Grandma Tyack would be entertaining her most important customers, who had come to settle their accounts, in the upstairs dining-room, with plum cake and sandwiches, while Jane entertained the less important ones to a fish tea in the kitchen. Grandma would be in her black silk gown and small black bead-embroidered apron, her grey hair, now rather scanty, drawn up into a bun and covered with a frilly starched lace cap. Grandma was short and stout. She was shrewd and proud and pompous. Her grip on the business was tight. She kept all business matters in her own hands. Grandma never forgot that she traced her lineage back to courtiers who came over from France in 1244, and were given lands in Cornwall.

On Saturday afternoons the children had to be dressed in their best bib and tuckers, the girls in white starched pinafores and the boys in fresh white shirts with their hair brushed back, to be presented to the important customers and pass round the tea and cake. It was "Yes, Mrs Berriman; Thank you, Mrs Richardson; How do you do, Mrs Thomas," or "Mrs Paul," and so it went on. Muriel reluctantly uncurled herself from the window seat and went down to join the others.

Tyack's was a prosperous business opposite the church. Three storeys high, the building dominated the main road entering Camborne. There were three shops below - ironmongery, saddlery and the first cycle shop in Camborne, all with large display windows. Above, there were six large bay windows. As well as the business premises, there were spacious living quarters for the family, eleven rooms in all. At the back there were a number of workshops which included plumbing, a blacksmith's shop and glass works. They also kept dynamite - it was said that the Tyacks kept enough dynamite to blow up the whole of Camborne. There were stables for the horses, and Tyack's back lane was famous because Richard Trevithick had tested his steam engine there. He was a close friend of the family and related to them by marriage through his sister. Behind all this bustle and activity lay a beautiful garden, said to be one of the loveliest in Camborne. (Now sadly all built over.) There were rare flowers and shrubs, fruit trees, an aviary and a greenhouse with luscious grapes. The children were allowed to play freely in the garden, pretending to be miners and digging their own shafts and tunnels. They each had their own flower patch, where they vied with one another to produce the most beautiful plants. On Saturdays, when the house was having a grand 'clean up' for Sunday, the children would take their pasties out into the aviary to eat.

Annie Muriel was the only child, out of nine, not to be born in the house above the shop. The premises were being enlarged and modernised at the time of her birth (15 July 1884), and the family moved temporarily into Bassett House, in Wellington Road. Her mother always blamed the fact that the new premises were not properly dried out for Muriel's ill-health. Muriel was the fifth child. The first had been still-born. Then there was handsome Harry, Muriel's champion at all times. Mabel came next; she was the only one with blue eyes and was bossy and self-opinionated, and from an early age she had decided to be a nurse. Leonard was the quiet one - he was more fond of his rabbits than of the games and parties the others enjoyed. After Muriel came George. He had the brains of the family, with a brilliant inventive mind, perhaps inherited from the Trevithicks. He was very generous, with great compassion for the under privileged. Katy was the Saturday child, loving and giving, who spent her life caring for others. Little Percy died at two years old from whooping cough. Willie, the youngest, had suffered a viral infection in pre-natal life. In those days there was no knowledge of the danger of viral infection to the foetus. In consequence, he was deaf, dumb and partially-sighted, and he also had a heart condition.

When Muriel was a toddler she burnt her hand badly on a hot iron carelessly left to cool on the tiled kitchen floor. In great distress, her father saddled his horse and galloped off to a nearby gypsy encampment and brought back a well-known healer, who touched her injured hand and it was healed almost at once, leaving no scar. Muriel was always proud of her long, sensitive, beautiful hands.

Camborne in the nineteenth century was a busy, lively town, a centre of mining. The Tyack children loved to look out of the upstairs window to the busy street below. There was the church with weddings and funerals to watch, what people wore and the horses and carriages. There was the market place with its stalls and the street vendors selling their wares. Tom Angove, the blind evangelist, and his wife Grace would set up a little table on which was placed his braille Bible, and he would exhort passers-by to turn from their wicked ways and be saved. In his fervour he would kneel in the mud and pray for their souls, until Muriel's mother took pity on him and gave him an old piece of carpet to kneel on.

The Tyacks were a happy, boisterous, fun-loving family. Brought up as staunch Methodists, they had a strict sense of right and wrong and were very conscious of the devil and all his works, but also of God's love and mercy. Muriel's Christian faith, learned in childhood, was the shining light in her life and never deserted her.

Theirs was an ever open door, no one in need was turned away, be they friend or stranger. Many years later, an old employee of theirs remarked that the poor of Camborne owed more to the Tyacks in their day than to anyone else. Muriel was afraid that her mother would give her last petticoat to Mrs Estlick, the umbrella woman, who came periodically to repair the family's large stack of umbrellas and, after drinking a nice hot cup of tea, would end with: "Mrs Tyack dear, I suppose 'ee 'aven't a petticoat to spare?" She never went away empty-handed.

They were not allowed to sit down to Sunday dinner until dinner was taken down the lane to the poor and needy. Each child had a special family allocated to them. Father might also bring a lonely soul or stranger from chapel to partake of the feast. Grace was sung before the family sat down to eat. There was always a large joint of beef, Yorkshire pudding, roast potatoes and a good supply of vegetables in season. In spite of the generous supply of food, with so many extra mouths to feed, Mother was sometimes afraid it would not go round, and would wipe away a silent tear.

All the children's plates had to be cleared; Father would not allow fads or waste. Jellies, custard and other sweets followed, with a plentiful amount of Cornish clotted cream. Games were not allowed on Sunday, the children went to Sunday school, learnt their text from the Bible, read good books only, and entertained their friends. In the evenings they sang hymns around the piano. Although by modern standards it seems very dull, it was a happy family day which they all enjoyed.

As a small child Muriel attended a Dame school run by the Misses Eliza and Annie Pengelly, daughters of a Falmouth sea captain. They had taken Bassett House, the house in which Muriel had been born. Twelve or fourteen small children would sit around a large table in a little room with only a small window, half hidden by a large flowering plant and seldom opened. They sat, writing and doing their sums on slates, and reading from their primers, from 9 am to 6 pm, with a break for dinner and no time for play. If one of the boys said a rude word, Miss Eliza would drag him, holding him firmly by the ear, to the kitchen, where Miss Annie, who did most of the housework, would wash out his mouth with mustard and water. Sometimes the boys would become restless and kick the girls under the table. Miss Annie would then take a strong cord and tie the offender's legs to the table. In his efforts to free himself he would sometimes knock over the table, everything would land on the floor and pandemonium would reign. At least it caused a diversion.

It was often more economical in a large family to employ a governess, so Miss Botterell, who had previously taught the Eva children, came to them. Her father had held a good position in Dolcoath tin mine (in which Mrs Tyack had shares) but had been killed in a disaster, leaving his wife in poor circumstances. Miss Botterell was very hard working and fun to be with. She stayed for some years and became part of the family. Her wages would not have been more than a pound a week; for that she taught the children the three R's and gave music lessons. The bigger ones would play on the piano in the drawing-room, and the small ones on the old schoolroom piano. Muriel was not particularly musical, but it became one of the great joys of little Katy's life. Miss Botterell would also help with the mending, take the children for long walks, and sit with Grandma and read the Bible to her. In winter she produced little plays for the children to act in, making the costumes herself. The audience was made up chiefly of Tyack's staff, and as they had about fifty employees, and the schoolroom was small, a number of performances had to be given. It was great fun and everyone enjoyed it.

Another highlight was the summer garden-fête, given by the children under the supervision of Miss Botterell. Entrance was a penny, and any child who did not have a penny could give a slate pencil. The money was given to some good cause. Miss Botterell was interested in the occult, and would sometimes have table-tapping sessions with the children. Their parents were horrified when they found out. At weekends Miss Botterell went home to Florence Villa, Roskear, where she worked harder than ever looking after her mother, and seemed glad to return on Monday mornings. Even after she married, became a widow and went to live in New Zealand, she continued to write most affectionate letters.

After Miss Botterell left, Muriel attended Redbrook Ladies College, where she excelled in English and loved writing essays. She also enjoyed history, like her mother, and loved drawing and painting. She was a good artist and attended the local Art School for some years. Muriel was always interested in people and the way they lived; being of curious nature, she would sometimes ring the bell of an interesting looking house on her way home from school, to ask for a drink of water as an excuse to see what wallpaper they had.

Muriel's best friends at school were Elsie Murdock and Mary Glasson. Elsie was a descendent of Richard Murdock, who invented gas lighting, and Mary married the Honourable Francis Grosvenor and later became Lady Ebury. They all remained life long friends. Mary and Muriel were very alike, except for the colour of their eyes, Muriel's being dark and Mary's blue. Francis Grosvenor, who was a student at the Camborne School of Mines, would sometimes mix them up and find he was chasing Muriel down the street instead of Mary.

Muriel's mother was a great reader. She often read the children to sleep. The family would read to each other around the fire on a winter evening. They were very much indebted to the recently opened Passmore Edwards library. Mr and Mrs Passmore Edwards were friends of the family, and the Tyacks were invited to the openings of several of his libraries. The Passmore Edwards libraries were forerunners of public libraries in several Cornish towns, and the spacious granite buildings housing them are still in use.

Muriel's mother was a keen member of the Antiquarian Society (probably the forerunner of the Old Cornwall Society), and anything old interested her. The Society would arrange outings to places of interest, and if these were at any distance, a wagon would be hired, and the ladies would pack delicious picnics in wicker baskets covered with spotless white cloths. These outings were red letter days. The drive through the countryside, with everyone laughing and talking, and sometimes a sing-song, were happy occasions. The visit would be to some ancient ruin, old church or Celtic cross. After a lecture and discussion on the site, with everyone scribbling away in note books, they would drive home in the dusk or starlight, tired but happy, with a good warm supper prepared by Jane waiting for them. There would be a lot of chat and comparing of notes before they tumbled into bed.

In the summer, if mother's dividends from the tin mines were good, a seaside holiday would be arranged. In bad years they had to content themselves with walks. Cornwall had not then been developed as a holiday resort. Newquay was a small fishing village where they could wear their old clothes and run wild without shoes or stockings; St. Ives was the same. They also went to Perranporth, but their favourite place was St. Mawes, with its castle, and ferry boat to Falmouth or steamer up the river Fal to Truro. A large empty house would be taken; it had to be large, because there were seven children, as well as various aunts, cousins and numerous friends. It would be 'Dear Mrs Tyack, can't I come and help with the children?' and kind Mrs Tyack had difficulty in saying no.

A few days before, a covered wagon would be sent ahead in the charge of two workmen and Jane to supervise, containing bits and pieces of old furniture - beds, tables and chairs, and also crockery, cutlery and bedding, and clothes packed in large tin trunks. Several weeks before, a bolt of navy blue serge would have been bought and yards of white tape; a dressmaker was employed for a week at 1/6 a day to make bathing costumes. The girls' costumes were all alike, high up to the neck and reaching down to the knees. They had sleeves with frills at the elbow, and there were frills at the knee, all trimmed with rows of white tape.

On the eventful day, mother, children, nursemaid Lilly, aunts, cousins and friends would pack into a wagon and set off. Leonard's rabbits had to come too. What fun and excitement it would be - far jollier than the modern car speeding down a motorway. As soon as they arrived, off would come shoes and stockings, not to be worn again, except on Sundays, until the holiday was over. They never knew who else might turn up, as invitations were handed out liberally to friends and employees before leaving; room was always found for one more. If beds ran out, Muriel might find herself sleeping in one of the tin trunks padded out with pillows.

Muriel was a delicate girl, who was kept in bed a good deal, suffering from colds, sore throats and chest complaints, which later developed into tuberculosis. But in spite of her poor health she had a great zest for life, and when well enough, enjoyed joining in her brothers' pranks. She was the first girl in the town to ride a bicycle. The ladies in the town would hold up their hands in horror. "Shame, a maid on a bicycle!" They also disapproved as being highly immodest the baggy serge bloomers her mother had made for her.

It was decided when Muriel was in her late teens, that a tonsillectomy might help to improve her health; this was a new operation and beyond the skill of the local surgeons, so arrangements were made with an eminent London surgeon, but before the operation could be carried out, it was thought necessary to remove all her teeth.

Grandma Tyack was getting very old. She could no longer keep reins on the business. She kept to her room. The children took it in turns to sit with her and read the Bible. She loved to talk of her family and of the past. Muriel, who found such recitals boring, would sometimes turn a somersault to relieve the monotony, and would be severely reprimanded by the old lady.

Grandma's two sons, John and Charles, had not been brought up to run the business. With foolish pride, she had brought them up as gentlemen. John lived in a big house in the best part of town. Aunt Myra, his wife, came from a wealthy family. There were one boy and two girls of the marriage. She was a haughty woman with fastidious tastes, who looked down on the large Church Street family with their boisterous ways, and thought it was so common to live over the shop!

One sunny day Grandma Tyack died. The curtains were drawn and the children dressed in black. On the same day, their beloved dog, Keeper, was lying in the sun in the street when he was run over and killed. To the children, that was the greater tragedy.

With Grandma's passing Tyack's was never quite the same.

2

A GRANDDAUGHTER'S MEMORY OF HER GRANDPARENTS: ELIZABETH AND CHARLES TYACK

In the corner of our breakfast-room sits my grandmother's old rocking chair. She rocked her babies sitting in it and now I rock my little grandson David in the same chair and we are contented and happy together. I remember my grandmother sitting in this chair, rocking and knitting grey wool socks on steel needles, a shawl across her shoulders, while she listened to the troubles of her many callers. Her face was a mass of wrinkles; she had a placid expression, a high forehead, her hair drawn up into a small bun on top, bright intelligent eyes and a generous mouth. She usually wore black. She was a large comfortable woman, who gave us a sense of peace and security. Her tremendous faith in God's goodness and mercy never failed her. In spite of bringing up a large family, she never seemed ruffled or in a hurry, and could see the funny side of things. She would laugh until the tears ran down her old cheeks.

Never a day passed without someone calling to see her. Being a business house, the door was always open, and they would call up the stairs. "Are you there, Mrs Tyack?" and up they would come. Auntie Katy, who lived with her mother, would be occupied in the shop downstairs. Granny usually sat in the dining-room on the first floor, which was connected to the kitchen below by a service lift. When we were children Auntie Katy would give us rides in this lift, which was pulled by hand. Being a nervous child, I was always terrified that the ropes would break. Up would come the caller with some little gift "Mrs Tyack dear, I've just made some buns and I thought you'd like a few," or "These are the first raspberries in the garden" or "the first roses". Granny was very much loved and a good listener. They would pour out their troubles to her while she sat quietly knitting, not saying a word but listening. When they had finished, she would sum up the situation in a few wise words. How rare it is to find someone who really listens.

When I was six my parents went to Trinidad. Because of my mother's TB, my father had been advised to take her to a warm climate, and Nadia went with them. My eldest sister, my brother and I were left in the care of Granny and Auntie Katy. Granny and I were very close - I was named after her - and we had a great affinity. I sat on a tufty at her feet and we would compose stories together or make pictures out of the dying embers. TV was not even thought of then. She would tell me of her secret, long ago romances, with the admonition that I must not tell Auntie Katy, who was rather prim.

Granny was born at Carharrack in the 1850s. Her father, Richard Goldsworthy, was a mine manager, or captain, as they were called. He was John Taylor's first agent for Cornwall, and well thought of in the mining world. Her uncle was the much loved Dr Mitchell of St. Day.

Of her mother I heard little. She died young, leaving two daughters and a son. She was related to John Williams who dreamt of the murder of the Chancellor of the Exchequer, Spencer Perceval, in the House of Commons in 1812. He dreamt repeatedly of this murder on the 3rd of May, although the murder did not take place until the 11th of May; he was also able from this dream, to recognise the murderer. (See *Man's Survival After Death* or *The Other Side of Life* by Charles F. Tweedale FRGS, Vicar of West Ocley, printed in London by Grant Richard, 1909.) Both my mother and grandmother inherited his psychic powers.

Her mother seemed a gentle soul, and the only story of her that I remember was that one day she and Granny, then a small child, were out walking and became tired; they begged a lift from a miner on a donkey 'shay'; just then Great-grandfather passed, with an important mine official down from London, and great was his annoyance and humiliation to see his wife and daughter riding on a donkey shay.

Granny was the eldest daughter. After their mother's death they were brought up by a rather unpleasant housekeeper who probably had enough wit to keep on the right side of the master, but showed little love to his orphaned children. My grandmother, who never held a grudge, looked after her in her old age. Her father, though a good and generous man, was rather severe, a very strict, puritanical early Methodist. Revival meetings would be held in the kitchen, when Granny would be tossed in the air to cries of "Alleluia, little Elizabeth," crinoline flying.

When there was a slack period in the mines, Captain Goldsworthy, Granny's father, set his miners to work enlarging Gwennap Pit - the famous preaching theatre where John Wesley preached and which is still in use today. On Sundays the only exercise allowed was the walk to chapel and back. No dishes were washed, and the mirrors were covered. The only books read were the Bible and *Pilgrim's Progress*.

In those days there was great fear of the French. Granny was terrified of invasion by the French, and naughty children were threatened with "If you don't behave, Boney [Napoleon] will get you!"

There were happy peaceful days playing in the fields with the lambs. Like Mary, Granny had a pet lamb which she used to dress in a bonnet. She told me of primroses and daisy chains, and of the little streams that meandered through the meadows where they would paddle on a hot day, and how one day she lost her shoe which was carried away by the stream. They would take their dolls to St. Martha's Well for baptism, and there was the day when her beautiful wax doll melted in the sun.

Granny's brother was a very religious boy who said long prayers in the privy midden. He went to boarding school, and died at an early age of typhoid fever. I used to wonder if the unhealthy atmosphere of the midden had contributed to his early death. She always had a great fear of boys' boarding schools, and was very upset when my brother was sent away to school. Her fears were justified when he was taken ill at school and died. Grandfather Charles was sent to boarding school in Yorkshire and was so unhappy there that he ran away and walked all the way back to Cornwall.

Her father was keen on education, and she stayed at school until she was eighteen. She used to tell me of her first Dame

School, where the boys' and girls' playgrounds were separated by a high wooden fence, which did not stop her little sweethearts throwing notes over the wall to her.

When she grew up she was the belle of the countryside and had many admirers; she lost her heart to one who emigrated to America. He asked her to come with him but the journey to America in those days was a long hazardous one, and her courage failed her. He made his fortune. I sometimes thought she regretted her lost love. She was rather proud: one day when she went to tea with friends she was given a cabbage; too ashamed to be seen carrying a cabbage, she threw it over the hedge. She would say to me: "Many a time in after years I wished I had that cabbage!"

Then Grandpa Charles came riding on horseback over from Camborne to court her. They were all strict teetotallers, but Grandpa's family had a housekeeper who was a secret drinker. One cold day Charles went to the kitchen cupboard to take what he thought was cough mixture, before riding over to see Elizabeth. She was horrified to smell alcohol on his breath and sent him away in disgust, much to his bewilderment. Eventually the misunderstanding was cleared up. Nicely brought up young ladies did not allow a man to kiss them before marriage, and Granny was no exception.

Elizabeth Bowden Goldsworthy married Charles Tyack on the 5th of February 1878 at Redruth Methodist Chapel. She wore a blue silk dress, with matching bonnet, trimmed with orange blossom and myrtle and a bridal veil. Her bridal bouquet was supplied by Tresidders of Truro, then already established for forty years, and a well known firm of nurserymen to this day. We still have their bill in our possession. There were two carriages, with two pairs of matching greys. There was a liberal wedding breakfast in her father's house, but no alcohol of any kind. Healths were drunk in cold water. Granny had twenty dresses in her trousseau, and I loved her to tell me about them.

Charles and Elizabeth left after the wedding feast by the 12 o'clock train to Plymouth,for a two week honeymoon. They also spent some time in Torquay and in Bath, where they visited the Roman Baths. The last week was spent in London. On Sunday they went in the afternoon to the great Queen Street Chapel, and in the evening to a Roman Catholic Church, which I find surprising in two such strict puritans. They visited many other places of interest - the British Museum, the South Kensington Museum, Westminster Abbey, Hyde Park, the Crystal Palace, the Zoological Gardens and the Royal Aquarium. The highlight of the visit was a conducted tour of the House of Commons by Mr James Hogg, MP. They were allowed to stay in the visitors' gallery for a sitting. They were also very amused by a visit to Madame Tussaud's.

Of Grandfather Charles I remember little, except as a rather peppery old gentleman, short in stature, with rosy cheeks, a beard and bright blue eyes. He would fall asleep in an armchair after midday dinner on Sundays, with a handkerchief over his face, and we would creep up behind him and try to pull it off, much to his annoyance. Granny always seemed to be the dominant one, the queen of the house. In his sixties he developed motor neuron disease, first dragging one leg and then becoming completely paralysed. They say that at his funeral the procession stretched down the whole street to the town clock and round the corner. Many people previously unknown to my grandmother came to her afterwards and told her how much they owed to her husband, and how he had helped them in times of need and set them on their feet. When the photographer down the street went bankrupt and the family was evicted, Grandfather put them all up in his premises until new accommodation could be found for them.

He was no businessman (probably because his mother had kept control of the business for too long in her own hands), and with so much poverty in the town, he was reluctant to press for payment when times were hard, and so the business declined.

His children loved him, and beneath the gruff exterior I saw as a child, was hidden a very kind heart. He could not bear waste of any kind and collected and hoarded anything which he thought might come in useful.

3

THE SARA FAMILY

William George Willoughby Sara was a tall elegant man with a good deal of charm. He had light blue, rather prominent eyes, aquiline features, a fair complexion, and when I first remember him, he was going bald, and wore a moustache which he later shaved off. Inclined to be highly-strung, he had an explosive temper; but on the whole he was a jovial fellow with a good sense of humour, who loved pleasant company.

Born the eldest son of a prosperous Truro jam manufacturer and corn merchant, with warehouses on the wharf and a fine house in Lemon Street, he had a comfortable middle-class home and a good education at King's College, Taunton. For a time he joined his father's business, but his lack of ambition and business drive led to a split in their relationship. His father bought him a sweet factory which did not succeed. When I first knew him he was working in the office of the dynamite factory near Gwithian, Hayle. He found his true vocation only in his sixties, when he became ordained as a priest in the Anglican church.

Willie, as he was better known, adored children and was always planning treats for them. He was a beloved grandfather to us, and we would seek in his pockets for sweets, which we invariably found. I remember one hot August day years later, when he took all the children from Madron Workhouse for an outing to Madron wishing-well and us along with them, supplying us all with oranges and chocolate. My first memory of him is when he and his family lived in a substantially built detached house called Chy-an-Towan, which is Cornish for the house on the sand hills.

He loved flowers, and was proud of his garden. He also kept pigs, and sometimes one would escape, and all the family would chase over the towans looking for it. As a boy he once had a pet pig, and was heart-broken when it was served up for dinner on Sunday, and refused to have any part of the meal.

On good days Grandpa would entertain us with comic songs from the music-halls. Two of his favourites were:

> Katy, my beautiful Katy,
> I'll be waiting for you at the kitchen door,
> When the moon shines over the cowshed I'll be there.

and

> Dan, Dan, funny old man
> Washed his face in a frying-pan
> Combed his hair with a cart-wheel
> And died with a toothache in his heel.

whereupon we would go into hoots of laughter.

Adah Sara was a complete contrast to her husband, but theirs was a successful marriage. She was the practical one, the stable one who kept the wheels turning, and, in spite of having only a small income, kept a good style and a beautiful, perfectly run home. She was petite and very proud of her tiny feet, on which she wore pretty size 2 shoes. She had brown eyes and a long Grecian nose. Her hair went white at an early age and she took great pride in dressing it in little waves high on her head. It was washed in borax once a week. Adah was the eldest daughter of William Clyma, a well known book and print seller in Truro and an alderman of the city. Among his clients he numbered Lord Tennyson. Her family had always been public benefactors; an uncle had started the Poor Law in Truro, and her great-grandmother was a well known Methodist and had played a large part in the founding of the Dorcas Society. Anna Reynolds' diary, given by my father to the Methodist Historic Society, is now in the city archives and is considered a valuable record of early Methodism in Truro.

As a girl Adah and her sister Janie were well grounded in the art of household management by their mother. Mrs Clyma died tragically, shortly before Adah's marriage. She was travelling to Perranporth in a horse-drawn omnibus when it caught alight; she was on the upper deck, and as she jumped down she caused herself an internal injury from which she died. It is said that she still haunts the Drosken - the high cliffs at Perranporth - which used to be her favourite walk. As wedding plans for Adah and William were by then well advanced, they were married quietly.

Adah was an accomplished artist; she also did exquisite embroidery and lace-like crochet. She was an excellent housewife and cook, a perfectionist in everything she did. I found her rather formidable, but I am grateful for the excellent training she gave us. She had four sons, all of whom adored her and put her on the highest pinnacle.

Percy, the eldest, died before I was born. He was tall and lanky, attractive in an ugly sort of way. He had a freckled face protruding ears and straight brown hair. He was a bit of a dandy, popular with the ladies and enjoyed a good time. He was an artist who drifted along in an easy going way. In his twenties he developed tuberculosis and was sent to California for health reasons. While there he seemed to be in very poor spirits at times. He was caught up in the San Francisco earthquake, and this, coupled with exposure, seemed to have precipitated his death. His father was warned of his death in a dream: he saw Percy carried on a stretcher, with blood gushing from his mouth.

Claude, the second son, was very different in looks and in character. He was short, but had very broad shoulders for his height He had been a delicate premature baby, and probably suffered from some degree of stunted growth. He had fair curly hair, light blue eyes, his mother's Grecian nose and a sensitive mouth. He was very hard working and ambitious. He had a brilliant scientific mind, but also a romantic side to his nature, and he wrote poetry. He was I think, the most honest person I have ever met, blunt and straightforward in speech, but he also had a deep sympathy for those in trouble, and a very gentle side for those he loved. He had a quirky sense of humour and could see the funny side of life. He did brilliantly at school and left early, after the headmaster told his father he could teach him no more. He then went to the Camborne School of Mines where he excelled.

Gerald, the third boy, was short and darker in colour. My father always said that Gerald was the cleverest of the four boys, but he did not have the same steadfastness of purpose that my father had, nor ambition. He became a mining engineer, metallurgist and research chemist. A great part of his adult life was spent in Canada. He enjoyed being in company with others, drinking and having a good time. He married May Carter, a Newfoundlander who came from old pioneer stock. Her family were given the privilege of flying the White Ensign for the part they played in defending Newfoundland from the French.

Teddy, or Edmund to give him his correct name, was the youngest of the family. As a small boy he had brown curls and big brown eyes, and was his mother's pride and joy, but his brothers thought of him as the fool of the family. In spite of this he became a priest in the Church of England and was later consecrated a bishop. He became Assistant Bishop first of Jamaica, then of Bath and Wells, and finally of Hereford, and Rector of Ludlow. He married Mary Butler, whom he met at the University in Dublin. She was a classics scholar. She was very beautiful, with corn coloured hair, blue eyes and a peach-like complexion. In spite of her beauty, as a child I thought of her as the Ice Queen, because of her reserved manner. Teddy became well known for his work with Sunday schools and youth movements; he also became a Christian psychiatrist and helped many through this branch of his work.

4

COURTSHIP AND MARRIAGE

The Tyack and Sara boys knew each other from an early age although they were not close friends. The children attended the same parties at Christmas. Claude did not become aware of Muriel until one day he saw her cycling down Trelowarren Street (the main shopping street), her hair flying. It was very unusual in those days to see a girl on a bicycle, in fact Muriel was the first girl in Camborne to ride one. Claude turned to the friend he was with and said, "*That* is the girl I intend to marry" - and he loved her until he died. About the same time, Muriel became aware of Claude, and she would persuade Elsie Murdock to take the long way home from school so that they passed Claude's home in Roskear, in the hope of seeing him. Claude and Muriel were at the time both at school - both clever children. Muriel, with artistic ability, obtained a prize for writing and was gifted in painting and drawing, and Claude had a brilliant mind.

Claude and Muriel's courtship was not without problems. Muriel's mother and Claude never really liked each other; because of his blunt manner she never recognised his true worth and preferred his brother Gerald who flattered her a little - she did enjoy a little attention. Muriel was allowed to receive Claude in the upstairs drawing-room, with the bay window overlooking the Church: but Mabel was always sent in to practise the piano and act as chaperone - an arrangement loathed by all of them. Mabel would say in later life:

"Claude never really liked me since Mother made me play 'Gooseberry'."

Claude's family on the other hand, thought him far too young to be seriously attached to anyone. Although less well-off than the Tyacks, they were proud, snobbish, and more 'exclusive'. They despised the Tyacks for 'being Chapel', for though brought up in Methodist families, they had joined the Church of England. They also looked down on the Tyacks for being 'in trade' and the way their door was always open to all, however dirty or destitute. The Saras were, to be fair, charitable people, but more reserved and circumspect. Muriel was a delicate girl and they did not like the way she spat up blood every now and then.

Claude was doing well at the School of Mines. By this time his family had moved to Hayle and he cycled the seven miles to Camborne and back, night and morning. On a certain place on Roseworthy Hill, he always experienced a sense of horror and a desire to 'turn tail' and cycle away as quickly as possible. Years later, he discovered that a gallows had once stood on that spot. The time came for the scholarship examination to The Royal School of Science at South Kensington. Claude was one of the youngest students and was not due to take this examination for at least another year. He begged Mr Berringer, the principal, to allow him to sit to gain experience, and he succeeded in passing - with honours - thereby winning a three year scholarship to South Kensington. Everyone was delighted with his success.

The only cloud was his parting with Muriel. During the long vacation, glorious sunny day followed sunny day. Muriel and Claude with a rucksack containing lunch - a pasty each, some saffron buns, and a bottle of lemonade or ginger-beer - would set off for the north cliffs. They walked through pleasant country lanes and then to the tin-steaming works where the Bal maidens were employed. They had to cross the murky red streams, balanced precariously on wooden planks. However, when they arrived at the north cliffs, they had one of the most spectacular cliff views in the world! They would crawl gingerly on their stomachs to look over Hell's Mouth at the foaming, curdling sea below, the cormorants and seagulls cawing and circling around. The climb down to the little sandy Fisherman's Cove was steep - but what a wonderful place! Sand, sea and sun, and two young people in love - an earthly paradise. Yellow sands with no footprints but their own. Tourists had not found their way to Cornwall in those halcyon days.

Another favourite place was Penpons Woods where Claude would read poetry to Muriel under the trees, while she made garlands of ivy to hang about their necks. One sunny day as they strolled on the cliffs, Claude asked Muriel if she would make their parting easier by becoming engaged before he went away. She happily consented. Theirs was a sweet, innocent love with no thought of sex before marriage. Claude took a piece of cotton thread to measure her finger for a ring. When he told his brothers that evening that he was engaged, they laughed at him, scorning: "Fancy getting tied up with a girl at your age when life is all before you for having fun!"

His parents were equally disapproving but Mother relented sufficiently to say, "Bring her to tea on Sunday."

An angel from heaven would not have been good enough for one of her boys and that skinny Muriel Tyack certainly wasn't - and a hoyden to wit, riding a bicycle! Muriel's parents were no better pleased.

In spite of family disapproval on both sides, Claude and Muriel were not deterred. Claude took his piece of cotton thread to Mr Wearne - the jeweller - and chose a ring for Muriel - five opals set in diamonds - on which he spent the prize money he had been given for buying textbooks. Her finger was so small that Mr Wearne asked if he was getting married to a child! The ring had to be enlarged twice through Muriel's lifetime. So - the young hopeful took a train to London and South Kensington, bound for honour and glory. The college had booked a room for him in a nearby boarding-house and he took a hansom cab to what was to be his home for the next three years.

Muriel and Claude found the parting very wearisome but they kept their promise to each other and corresponded daily throughout the whole three years. Claude proved an excellent - in fact brilliant student, passing all his examinations with Honours. He had an enquiring mind and did a great deal of research - in fact there was no branch of science studied by him in which he did not make a new discovery! Whilst studying the cause of malignant disease in plants, he found a difference in cell structure and he concluded that a predisposition to cancer was found in the cell structure of the individual or plant. He was about seventy years before his time, as the medical profession are now only starting to consider this line of thought.

In the meantime, Muriel spent some time working in the office of her father's business. Her hobby was painting, and she attended the local art school. Mrs Sara invited Muriel to stay at Hayle from time to time in order to get to know her better, and to train her for the responsibility of being Claude's wife. The Saras enjoyed a good social life and Muriel was taught the art of genteel entertaining, It was all a far cry from the hurly burly and happy-go-lucky ways of her own big family.

Claude's brothers became very fond of Muriel. She represented for them, the sister they had never had, and she became their confidante. Having four brothers of her own, she was well used to boys and their ways. They enjoyed escorting her to parties and picnics in Claude's absence and when in Camborne, made a habit of dropping in to the Tyacks. Little Katy struck up a friendship with Teddy whom she greatly admired for his romantic good looks!

At this time Mabel was training as a nurse at the Royal Bristol Infirmary, and little Willie was attending a boarding school for the deaf and dumb. George was a student at the Camborne School of Mines where he displayed a brilliant, creative mind. He was to become a mining engineer. Muriel's health was becoming worse during Claude's absence in London - she was coughing badly and spitting up more blood. Dr Tonkin diagnosed that his favourite patient had Consumption and both families set their face against a marriage. In spite of it all, Claude and Muriel's letters at this time show that they believed that their love would overcome all difficulties and perhaps, in another year, the families would become reconciled to their union. Another 'bone of contention' between the two sets of parents, was that the Saras were 'Church' and the Tyacks 'Chapel'.

Claude was approaching the end of his three years at university. As well as study, he found the various aspects of London life quite fascinating, and in later life loved to recall the excitement of Mafekin night! He passed his final examinations with Honours and was made an Associate of The Royal College of Science (A.R.C.S.) and only missed being made a Doctor because he had not matriculated at school. This had been a new examination when he was a boy and it had seemed unnecessary to his headmaster - "something new-fangled".

The university offered him a research bursary, and although he would have found it most interesting, he declined because due to his long-sight, microscopic work was causing a great deal of eye strain - and also he wanted to get married! In order to be near Muriel therefore, he took a post as instructor at the Camborne School of Mines for a temporary period. Muriel's health was giving more and more anxiety. Dr Tonkin gave her only six months to one year to live. Claude was more than ever determined that they should marry and have what life they could together. He was offered, and took, a post in the Mendip Hills in Somerset as manager of a small coalfield. He travelled to Somerset and found a flat for himself and Muriel in a charming farmhouse (Southwell House, at Ubley, West Hartley) with a motherly farmer's wife, explaining that his wife-to-be was very sick and would need careful nursing. The day before he was due to leave for the wedding, he received a telegram from Muriel's mother to say she was too ill to be married - but he would not be put off.

Harry travelled down from Scotland with Lilies of the Valley for her wedding bouquet - but where he found Lilies of the Valley in Scotland in February, is a mystery! Mabel was given leave from the Royal Infirmary to attend the wedding and bought herself a beautiful white silk dress with lace insertions for the occasion. When Mother saw it, she decided that it was more suitable for the bride, and that Muriel should wear it - much to Mabel's resentment.

Claude and Muriel were finally married on the 26th of February 1906 in the ancient church of St. Martin's. She was given away by her brother Harry who had joined the Church of England and had always been her 'champion'. The vicar said it was the prettiest wedding he had ever seen in the church. Their parents still did not approve of their 'foolhardiness' and, in protest, Claude's father refused to attend the ceremony. Claude was twenty-three and Muriel twenty-one. Wrapped well in warm clothes and rugs, Claude carried his bride by train to Somerset in a reserved carriage. Their wedding photograph was taken some time later when Muriel's health had improved.

On arrival at West Hartley, they were warmly welcomed by Mrs Richards - the farmer's wife. Muriel was put straight to bed and nursed lovingly by Claude. There was a fire in her room night and day. The window looked out on peaceful Somerset countryside. Everything was kept spotlessly clean by Mrs Richards and her 'apple-cheeked' maid Nancy. Nancy was about Muriel's age and they enjoyed a chat and laugh together. Muriel was given nourishing meals served daintily on a tray, with plenty of meat, eggs, cream, milk fresh and warm from the cow, and fruit and fresh vegetables. Mrs Richards was an excellent cook.

With rest, good food, and most important of all, surrounded and enfolded by Claude's tender love, Muriel's health improved, and as the days lengthened she was able to go and sit in the small cheerful sitting-room, looking out on the garden bright with spring flowers. When the warm weather came, Claude would carry her out to the orchard and place her tenderly on a couch under the trees. He could write verses or read to her. As well as being a brilliant scientist, Claude was a poet and had a romantic and passionate nature. Because of his deep love and Muriel's sickness, he restrained his strong sexual urges. Muriel was an 'innocent' when they married. In those days, girls went to their marriage bed with no instruction or knowledge of what sex entailed. The shock on a modestly nurtured girl could mar their marriage. Claude with his great sensitivity, gently wooed her into the art and joy of love-making.

During the day, Muriel was left in the care of the Richards, while Claude was busy at the mine. He delighted in bringing her small presents - a bunch of flowers, a book, or some other little luxury. He also liked to tease her a little. One day when digging on the Mendip, the miners came across the skeleton of a young girl - thousands of years old, but perfectly preserved. Her hair was still bright gold and had continued to grow after death until it surrounded her like a cloak. Claude pocketed a handful of hair, intending to tease Muriel about a blonde girlfriend - but by the time he reached home, the hair had turned to ashes in his pocket!

As Muriel's health began to improve, she put on weight and even grew a few inches so that her ankles showed beneath her skirts - much to the disgust of her mother-in-law who insisted that all her clothes should be lengthened. Muriel loved people and as she steadily grew better, she soon made friends and began to enter into the life of the community. They took great pride in arranging their wedding presents and setting up their first home. Teddy came to stay for a few days and thought it all very jolly. They also enjoyed entertaining other young people and their home was full of love and laughter. Claude joined the local tennis club and looked very handsome in his white flannels! Muriel would watch, sitting under a leafy tree protected by a large hat decorated with roses and a parasol. As the days grew shorter, they enjoyed cosy evenings by the fire. Claude would read poetry to Muriel while she sat on the hearthrug with her head against his knee.

But alas, those happy carefree days were soon to end.

5

SEPARATION

In November 1906, Claude, who was making quite a name for himself as a bright young man, received a letter from John Taylor of The Tasmanian Gold Company Limited, asking him to solve the problem of flooding in one of their mines in the Tamar region of Tasmania. He was offered a year's contract at the handsome sum of £200 a year. It seemed a fortune to them and too good an offer to miss. Unfortunately, as much of his time would be spent under canvas on the field, he was advised not to take Muriel. It was a heart-breaking decision to make. Muriel's health had greatly improved with all the love and attention she had received - but she put a good face on it, saying she would spend the time visiting family and friends.

Mrs Richards said she would keep the flat for them and see that it was well dusted and aired.

The days flew by - buying clothes and packing. The night before Claude left for Tasmania, he and Muriel knelt in prayer to ask for God's protection and help during their separation. They opened the Bible at the beautiful ninety-first Psalm

> 'He who dwelleth in the secret place of the
> Most High shall dwell under the shadow of the
> Almighty.'

This was an inspiration to them and sustained them throughout the whole of their lives. Whenever they were separated, it became a rule of life that on Sundays at 8.00 pm (British time) they would join together in prayer and repeat the ninety-first Psalm.

On December 18th, three days after his twenty-fourth birthday, Muriel waved good-bye to Claude as she saw him off on the boat-train. It was a cold bleak morning and Tasmania seemed a long way away. They clung together and tears streamed down both their faces. Great was their anguish on parting.

Harry, her favourite eldest brother, put his arm around her and tried to comfort her as he gently led her away. He hailed a cab and took her back to his comfortable bachelor flat. He tucked her up in a comfortable chair and made her a cup of tea. neither of them spoke - their feelings were too deep for words.

At that time, Harry was working at the famous warehouse - Cooks & Sons of St. Paul's Churchyard - in order to gain experience which would be of value when he returned to the family business. Harry had great charm and with his handsome good looks was a great favourite with the ladies whose company he enjoyed, although he had no desire to settle down with any one of them. He would say: "I could not bear to wake up every morning and find the same face on my pillow."

He had an eye for beauty and collected some rare and lovely pieces. He had renounced the Methodist tradition of the Tyacks and had become an Anglo-Catholic. The beauty and ritual appealed to his aesthetic taste; but he also had deep and sincere faith and a genuine caring for others.

Muriel spent a few days with Harry in his flat in order to recover from the ordeal of parting with Claude, before travelling to Yorkshire to spend Christmas with Aunt Fanny. She did some shopping and was thrilled with the bright lights and dazzling Christmas displays. Harry took her to the theatre to try to take her mind off things, and was very proud to show off his beautiful sister.

Claude's aunt Fanny Bell was a bright bustly little lady. She was short, plump, and motherly with soft brown hair arranged in a bun on top, rosy cheeks, twinkling blue eyes, and a generous mouth. She had written to Muriel, 'Come to us for Christmas and stay as long as you like. Father and the girls will love to have you - you will be as welcome as the flowers in spring; and that's saying something on a cold winter's morning in Yorkshire.'

Aunt Fanny was married to the Reverend Frederick Bell, Superintendent Methodist Minister. They lived in Westley House,

Skipton, Yorkshire. Uncle Fred was a jovial man with a square shaped face, a square shaped beard, and sideburns, a ruddy complexion, dark hair and eyes. He was a well known preacher, and in great demand at anniversaries and harvest festivals. A blunt, cheerful, no nonsense Yorkshireman, he ruled his family and circuit with kindness and firmness.

The Bells had four daughters and one son. Freda, the eldest, was tall and angular, and had intelligent bright eyes behind spectacles. She had a good head on her and she assisted her uncle in the well known travel agency - Bells of Bristol - travel agencies being a new-fangled idea at that time. Elsie was a teacher in her first post, later to become headmistress of a large girls' school. Hilda was delicate and stayed at home to become Mother's 'right hand'. Muriel, commonly called "Mu", had just left school and was still under Mother's eye. She was plump, pretty, and full of fun and laughter - the only girl to get married and become the mother of sons. Willoughby, the baby referred to as "Boy", was the pet and darling of them all. He was a boarder at King's School, which was a good thing, otherwise he would have been utterly ruined by his adoring mother and sisters.

When Muriel arrived at Westley House, they were all home for Christmas. Westley House was four square and solid, with a garden front and back. It was furnished with good solid mahogany furniture which was all clean and polished for Christmas. Yorkshire folk love their food and are famous for their hospitality. The table would groan with good things. Weeks before Christmas, Aunt Fanny would start planning for the great festival. Large joints of beef, ham, and tongue were ordered to be pickled down. Many pies and cakes were baked and Aunt Fanny baked a very rich Christmas cake. Fearing her family might want to sample it before Christmas, she baked a less rich one for every day use. She went in search of a cookery book she had recently bought at a bazaar for sixpence, compiled of various ladies' favourite recipes and sold to aid chapel funds. After studying many recipes, she decided on one called York cake. Never did a cake look such a success! It rose and it rose! It came up like a balloon and Aunt Fanny put it in her largest tin. "It looks so handsome we will keep it for Christmas," she said. "It should be called 'Royal' cake."

One afternoon, one of Uncle Fred's young ministers called to see him and was asked to stay for tea - so the York cake was taken out of its tin. The family were all told that on no account were they to ask for a piece. It looked very tempting on a high glass dish with a pretty handmade doily. Aunt Fanny pressed all the other good things on the young minister but never the York cake which he kept looking at with eyes of admiration, Finally he plucked up the courage to say:

"Could I have a piece of that cake please?"

So poor Aunt Fanny had to cut it! After the first bite he seemed to play with it on his plate, and with an effort, ate a few more mouthfuls. As the cake had already been cut, all the family wanted a piece . . . sawdust could not have tasted drier than that cake! No wonder it had risen so high - it had nothing in the way of goodness to keep it down!

Aunt Fanny knew it was useless to put it out for tea again and she hated waste, so she had a 'brainwave' - the Manse had a large wash house. A few days before Christmas it was given a good scrub out and rows of wooden forms were placed there. One would have thought that Uncle Fred was to hold one of his many services there. Amongst Aunt's many orders for Christmas was an oxtail. This, with many other nourishing things, she would put into her largest boiler on her huge Yorkshire range, and boil for hours to make good soup to give to the beggars, who came to the bake door at Christmas time. She thought that a good basin of hot nourishing soup with a chunk of her home-made bread would do them more good than money. They would sit on the forms to eat it, warmed by an oil heater. The soup was so good that they would come back day after day and bring their friends. Aunt Fanny's 'brainwave' was that she would change the menu and instead of soup, she would give them cocoa and a piece of York cake. The beggars came once, but none of them came back for more or brought their friends . . . never had Aunt Fanny been so free from beggars!

Muriel was accepted as one of the family. In fact, one of Uncle Fred's congregation asked Aunt Fanny if the tall beautiful girl was one of her daughters. She replied, "No - that is Mrs Sara."

"Never!" replied the woman, "she only looks like a girl."

6

TASMANIA

The blue-green depths of the Indian ocean, like a sheet of glass, spread for mile after mile. In the last 6,500 miles they had only sighted land three times and seen one ship. They were eight days out from Port Said and heading for Colombo. Claude was still feeling groggy after an attack of influenza. The ship's doctor had dosed him with quinine and called him "lad". They all thought of him as about eighteen. Claude was sitting on deck writing a long letter to Muriel - one of those 'newsy' letters that she could pass around to family and friends - not one of the intimate letters that were for her eyes alone where he poured out his love for her. Oh God - how he missed her! He wrote he had found Marseille dirty and depressing. In the Bay of Biscay it had been very rough - all front and back motion - no roll. Great big swells and strong head-wind with the sun almost vertically overhead. He had fallen in love with Naples.

There was a long account of his visit to Port Said. They had not docked until 4 pm so it had been a scramble to see as much as they could. The town was teeming with life; a mixture of wealth and squalor. Beggars and naked children lined the gutters. The guides almost knocked one over as they demanded about 100 times the price they expected to get for their services. They visited a mosque and a Buddhist temple. The flowers were beautiful and he wished he could send some home to Muriel who loved flowers so much.

As he wrote, two whales were sporting away in the distance and the flying fish looked very pretty dancing from wave to wave.

It was the hottest day they had had. On Monday they should be at Colombo and he was looking forward to going ashore.

The Captain and Officers belonged to the Naval Reserve and so *The Orient* flew the Blue Ensign instead of the Red, and they were very proud of themselves. The Captain and Second Officer had both married a few days before sailing and spent the time moping around. There was some mystery about the Quarter master who had for some reason, been reduced from the rank of Captain. He had connections with people in Camborne and Claude enjoyed a yarn with him.

The passengers were a friendly, jolly crowd. The crew organised many activities - bridge tournaments, whist-drives, quoits and a fancy dress ball amongst them to help relieve the monotony of the long voyage. There had been the usual fun on crossing the equator. Claude's letter went on with a vivid description of the passengers on his deck. There were two Roman Catholic priests on board and they enjoyed the fun with the others. There were quite a lot of Australians and Claude learned a good deal of Australian politics. They greatly admired Keir Hardy.

Claude had a comfortable cabin and had made it quite homelike with family photographs about; but in spite of the friendly company and fun, the journey seemed endless and he longed to reach Freemantle.

So the letter continued for fourteen pages. As the ship was considered British territory, the postage to any part of the Dominion was one penny!

Claude arrived in Abbeyfield on 25th January 1907. His letters of the 26th and 27th from Abbeyfield, Tasmania, described the gold mining town of about 4,000 inhabitants. It was a straggly town, made up of wood and corrugated houses with one or two brick built ones. It was generously supplied with places of worship of all creeds, but they were only attended by about sixty of the inhabitants. There was also a generous supply of pubs which were much better attended, but it was illegal to visit them on Sundays and anyone foolhardy enough to break this law, was fined £20. There was a newsagent who sold papers and out-of-date London periodicals. It also supported a lending library where a book could be borrowed for three pence. It had a reasonable selection.

On the way out, after landing at Freemantle, Claude had spent a few days in Melbourne at Scotts Hotel, before crossing to Tasmania. It was a wonderful relief to be on dry land and to have reached his destination. The company had booked him in at the Club Hotel - the best that Abbeyfield could offer. It was clean and comfortable but not the 'Grand' and to his great joy, he had a corner room with three windows and a sunny balcony with magnificent views over the surrounding countryside. The landlord and his wife - Mr and Mrs Dowling - did their best to make him feel at home. Opposite the hotel was the local theatre where very amateurish plays were produced. Mrs Dowling tried to persuade Claude to attend but he declined, preferring to read Shakespeare and write poetry.

Claude soon entered in the social life of the community and became very popular; but his heart was with Muriel in far-away England. He wrote that Mr Heathcot - the managing director of the company was friendly and helpful. He had been to the Camborne School of Mines in 1887. His sister, a plump, fresh faced girl of about twenty-five, lived with him. Mr Taylor - the chief engineer - and his charming wife, made him welcome. They had a delightful two-year-old daughter who made great friends with Claude. Mr Tanner - the vicar - invited him to the vicarage and they enjoyed each other's company. His best friends and the centre of social life in the community, were the Grahams - a big, jolly family where he was always welcome and spent most Sundays. Dr Graham he described as a bluff, open-hearted sort of man - one of four doctors in Abbeyfield.

Mrs Graham was a beautiful, cultured woman of Spanish descent. She had travelled widely and spoke fluently in English, French, Italian, Spanish and Greek - but preferred French. She and Claude had a common interest in their love of Greek mythology. There were four lively daughters who arranged tennis parties, picnics, whist-drives, dances and musical evenings. Claude became an enthusiastic member of the tennis club.

Abbeyfield was twenty-seven miles from the nearest train at Launceston. A motorcar travelled there and back twice a day - otherwise the only means of transport was by bicycle, horse, or on foot. Most of Claude's working life was spent in the region of the river Tamar - so called by the large colony of Cornish miners who settled there. The pits' manager, a Camborne man, had been in Tasmania since 1873 and was delighted to talk to someone who had only left Camborne six weeks before. The underground-manager - Mr Andrews - was a Redruth man. They called one side of the river 'Cornwall' and the other 'Devon'. Many places had been given west country names. Tasmania reminded Claude very much of England except for the vegetation.

The Tamar was a beautiful river.It had many tributaries and wooded banks, it reminded Claude of the river Fal. Claude's working life was very hard; as well as solving the drainage problem in the mine, he was surveying and making maps of the area. In a letter home he wrote, 'I have mapped 300 square miles of country in the last eight weeks. Not bad as the going was very hard.'

Much of the time was spent under canvas in the bush. Travelling on foot, cutting his way through bush six feet high, his travels took him to the picturesquely named 'Cabbage Tree Hill'. Alone in the bush, sleeping in a sleeping bag, cooking over a camp fire in a billy can with candles for light, it was a lonely life. He missed the comforts of home and family and in his desolation, Muriel became a dream person, a fantasy, a goddess of beauty and goodness. At weekends, he returned to Abbeyfield to collect his mail, have a bath, a change of clothes, go to church and enjoy the hospitality of Doctor Graham's family. Sometimes he made his headquarters at Westbury, staying at the Berriedale Hotel - a substantial stone built structure, well run by a jovial Irishman named J.P. Maloney. As a contrast to the bleakness of Abbeyfield, Westbury was a well established community with the charm of an English village, set in beautiful countryside.

The 1st of May heralded in winter and cold weather. The nights were bitter. On June 1st he described in his letter home a grand masked fancy dress ball. Claude described his own costume, designed by him, and his landlady helped him with the sewing. It was that of a medieval troubadour - piebald in red and green sateen. He filled two billy cans - one with red and one with green dye - to colour his stockings. He made a high pointed hat with red and green ribbons on which were sewn bells, with one attached to the point. There were also bells attached to the sleeves. A long cloak in green, lined with red, completed the outfit. Claude was very proud of his achievement and felt like a peacock!

Claude wrote that Mr Tanner was dressed as "Old Nick" with horns, claws and a tail! Mr Heathcot was a Spanish inquisitor. He looked so awful that his sister who did not recognise him, refused to dance with him. Mr Valentine, the bank manager, told his wife that he was not going, and then dressed up as a tramp. He decided to try his 'disguise' out by calling on his best friends who turned him away - and even the dog did not recognise him! He then called at another house and was offered tucker. At the dance, he asked his wife for a dance and she said, "Go away you horrid man," and then turned to a friend and said, "I don't know how such a disgusting creature got in. I am glad he is not my husband!"

After enjoying his joke, he went home and then returned, looking very smart in full evening dress. Doctor Graham's daughters looked very pretty - one as Dolly Varden, one as a Persian lady dressed in baggy trousers all pink silk and floating white muslin. Another was dressed as a French fishergirl. The prize went to a girl dressed as a gypsy. Claude escorted the gypsy and 'Dolly Varden' to supper - one on each arm. He always had an eye for a pretty face and enjoyed female company; but he loved only Muriel.

His letters home at this time were full of longing for England. The winter was cold and wet, conditions were hard and difficult. Often Claude was wet through as he struggled against the elements. The spartan conditions were very trying for one who loved beauty and comfort. It was a great relief when the days became longer and warmer.

On 15th December, Claude celebrated his twenty-fifth birthday. He wrote in his letter that he felt that the days of his youth were behind him; and due to so much study, he had had no real boyhood. Christmas day was glorious, warm and sunny. The Grahams arranged a picnic which everyone enjoyed.

During Claude's stay in Tasmania, his work came to the notice of the Tasmanian government and they were so impressed that they offered him the post of government geologist, which he declined.

On 25th January 1908 he wrote: 'I am leaving Abbeyfield in half an hour and not sorry to be going.' A few nights previously, the Grahams had given a farewell party for him in the form of a musical evening. He was sorry to say good-bye to the many friends he had made and who had shown him so much kindness. Amongst the friends, mention should be made of a young man called 'Penny' who had come out straight from Camborne mining school where he had been a friend of Claude's brother Gerald. Claude and Penny very much enjoyed each other's company and were to meet again years later in Russia.

After leaving Abbeyfield, Claude describes a few hours in Launceston, watching a tennis match between Abbeyfield and Launceston, and saying a final good-bye to some of his friends before sailing on the *London* for Australia. He spent a week in Australia enjoying the sights and staying once more at Scotts Hotel in Melbourne. He made friends with a group of explorers who were planning an expedition into the then unexplored parts of Australia. This was an adventure after Claude's heart, and it was with great regret that he refused their offer to join them. Such a hazardous undertaking would have been unfair to Muriel.

The journey to England was long and tedious. It seemed endless - but he was going home! He arrived back in late March 1908. Great was his joy of reunion with Muriel.

In the meantime, after leaving Aunt Fanny's comfortable home. Muriel spent some time in Somerset before returning to Cornwall. Her cousin Maud Andrews had opened a business in Bridgwater. Maud was a widow with two children, Walter and Winnifred (later to become Mrs Norman Phillips). Maud was very sad and lonely. She was kind to Muriel and they found mutual comfort from one another. Winnie was a lively, affectionate child who gave Muriel a great deal of pleasure. Maud had a great fondness for Harry and offered him a partnership in the business for £1,000 when he left St. Paul's Churchyard. Harry had reservations about accepting the offer as he feared the contract might include marriage. Not only was Maud older than Harry, but he did not want to marry anyone; however, they settled for friendship and he eventually accepted her offer on a business level.

On return to Cornwall, Muriel divided her time between Camborne and Hayle. Claude begged her to spend her time with his parents as he was afraid that in a draughty business-house she might catch a chill and have a return of her old trouble. She missed the fun and happy-go-lucky ways of her own family, and was very lonely. It was very dull at Hayle, her mother-in-law was very exacting and critical. The three eldest Sara boys were abroad and Teddy at college. Mr and Mrs Sara were going through a period of financial difficulty and Claude thought that Muriel's contribution could be of help to them in more ways than one. Muriel did her best to cheer up the lonely couple but had many a quiet weep in the wash-house.

Gerald was working in the copper mines in Peru as a mining engineer. Percy was in California. It was hoped that the warm climate would help to cure him of his tuberculosis. He was an artist and scraped a living fruit picking.

In June Muriel spent a holiday in London with Harry before he returned to Cornwall, having completed his apprenticeship at Cooks. Muriel was full of vivacity and always tried to get as much as possible out of life. Harry said she would make an old man of him the way she dashed around, and Mother, in Cornwall, was so relieved when she arrived home in one piece.

Some notes written by her read as follows:

Friday June 1st 1907:	Arrived in London. Met by Harry.
Saturday:	Went to the Tower. On our way saw Tower Bridge open. Went to St. Paul's, St. Margaret's, All Hallows, Barking, Houses of Parliament and Lords. The National Art Gallery, Kensington Palace. Caught in the rain - 'bunked' home as quickly as possible.
Sunday:	Went to All Hallows, Southall. Mr Trapps came to tea and supper.
Monday:	Went to Greenwich - saw the Painted Hall, the Observatory and had tea there. Took the steamboat up the Thames to Charing Cross. Went to Westminster Abbey, saw the Waxworks and the Roman Catholic cathedral.

In August there was a meeting of the 'clans' at Hayle. Muriel's mother, Harry, Katy and Mabel (home from Bristol Royal Infirmary) were all staying at 'Taylors', now the 'Bluff Hotel' on Hayle towans. Walter Andrews and some friends were camping nearby and Teddy was home from college. They had splendid picnics on the beach. Muriel, staying with her in-laws, was the life and soul of the company. At night she wrote to Claude by candlelight and her pillow was wet with tears.

One cold wet day Muriel and Mabel went paddling in the rain with their umbrellas up. Mabel walked into an unseen pool and Muriel shrieked with laughter to see Mabel standing up to her waist in water - and with her umbrella up! Mabel did not see the joke.

The autumn and winter were long and dreary. Harry had departed for Bridgwater. Katy and Walter Andrews were in love but the family were opposed because they were cousins and Walter was thought to be a bit unreliable.

Muriel spent Christmas of 1907 quietly with Claude's parents at Hayle, at his request.

In March 1908 Muriel rented a small house at Gwithian - 'Sunny Bank' and prepared for Claude's return. She travelled to Southampton to meet him. It was a joyous reunion. They spent a few days in London as Claude had some business there, before returning to Cornwall.

It must have been wonderful to be together again. It was a glorious spring, two people in love - like the honeymoon they never had. The sun seemed to shine especially for them. They would pack lunch - pasties or sandwiches, saffron cake, and a bottle of lemonade or ginger beer, and set off for the cliffs or the beach. The north cliffs, Hell's Mouth, Fisherman's Cove, or Gwithian were favourite haunts. They walked for miles on the springy turf and sunbathed on the sands. Claude was a very strong swimmer and continued to swim into his eighties. He was well aware of the dangerous undercurrents on the north coast - there was not a yard of the beach he did not understand and he knew not to take risks.

The Electrical Company commissioned him to do a geological survey of the area around Hayle estuary and Muriel played the part of his 'assistant'.

Claude obtained a temporary post as lecturer at Camborne School of Mines, but money was getting short and the urge for new discoveries was strong!

7

EGYPT

In October 1909 Claude was offered the post of geologist and surveyor by Grahams of London, to work in the Gulf of Suez for the African Prospecting Syndicate. It was an interesting assignment with good prospects and although he was sad to leave Muriel again, it was an offer that could not be missed. It was unthinkable to take Muriel with him to camp in the heat and sand of the desert. She was in the early stages of pregnancy and needed all the care and comfort she could get.

On 11th October 1909 he wrote to his parents before sailing from the port of London:

> This ship is little more than a cargo ship, but I have a comfortable cabin. Uncle Fred Sellick came to the dock to see me off. I would not allow Muriel to come as it would be too dirty and tiring for her. I am quite excited and have bought a guidebook and maps of Egypt. Please look after Muriel for me or see that she is looked after.

On 30th November he wrote from the Hotel de Sinia: 'Sinia is best described as an animated pigsty!' His permanent address was: Zeita, c/o Messrs. Beyto and Company, Suez. The name 'Zeita' is derived from the Arabic word for oil. Claude was to move from camp to camp and to develop a great sympathy for the children of Israel and their forty-years' wandering in the desert. The Bible came alive to him as he visited many places mentioned in the Old Testament.

Claude and Muriel Sara, 1906.

The Tyack children.
Leonard, Harry, Mabel, Minnie (cousin), George and
Muriel in go-cart. Keeper the dog underneath.

Charles Tyack.

Elizabeth Tyack.

The Tyack family. Back row: Leonard, Mabel, George, Muriel, Harry. Front row: Willie, Mother, Katy, Father.

Edmund and William Sara.

Adah Sara.

Percy Sara.

Gerald Sara.

Muriel Sara and Ia (14 months).

Captain Richard Henry (Harry) Tyack, 1918.

Muriel Sara with children and the manager of
the oil fields in Russia.

Maikop oil fields, South Russia.
Inspection by Russian officials.
Claude Sara left front, including John Templeton.

Three sisters. Back row: Katy Tyack, Muriel Sara, Mabel Tyack, Ia Sara.
Front row: Betty Sara, Nadia Sara (baby), Lewis Sara.

Muriel Sara, 1923.

Lewis, Ia and Betty Sara.

On Christmas day, he wrote to Muriel:

This has been the most miserable day of my life and I have just eaten the most miserable Christmas dinner. The food was all right in the traditional manner but I was alone and it tasted like sawdust. I could hardly swallow it because you were not there.

Mr John Wells - his direct superior and chief engineer, was a man of great character and charm. He was most helpful to Claude who grew to have great respect for him. Claude wrote home that the natives almost worshipped Mr Wells. The second-in-command was a Cornishman - Captain Trefusis - whose brother lived near Falmouth.

On 9th January 1910 Claude wrote from the Sinai desert:

I am really camped in the above place now and it is almost the most desolate region I have ever seen - nothing but a great pebble waste with a few shrubs of tarfa or manna. Sweet, I would like to write poetry to you but am like those who sat by the rivers of Babylon and said, "How can we sing to the Lord in a strange land." You, sweet, are the queen of my dear homeland. I cannot sing of love dear and I dare not sing of sorrow lest I fill both our hearts with deeper pain. In this land there is no love or poetry but only hard, stern, nakedness of life. Here indeed, is the Valley of Bones! It is a 'dead' land which flaunts its bones like a skeleton. No wonder Arab myths deal with jinn and gouls - not the happy 'fairies' of St. Ia's land (St. Ives). Here one sees no fairies dancing in the swaying rushes, or playing in the thyme turf, but gaunt, dread demons in the swirling sand columns as they blow along. Here one never wants to stop and linger for all along one sees the sign 'To stop is death'. No groves or dells to fill one with the joy of life, but deep cut gorges ever talk of tombs. It is true that the country has a weird beauty of its own, a fascination, but it is the beauty of a vampire that if you begin to admire you are forever lost. At night the moonshine on the silver landscape has a magical quality. I often think that the last judgement day will be held here. It is a fitting place for the future revelations of God as it has been for those in the past. It seems very fitting that the great religions of the past have had their origin in this awful shadowless land where nothing can be hidden.

Claude was nearly three years making maps and surveying for oil in the Gulf of Suez - some of the maps he made were used in the First World War. He moved from camp to camp during that time and became on good terms with the Arabs. He maintained order and good work by fining their head man if they misbehaved - a system which worked well and which they respected. The chief sheik of five tribes became a special friend of his and invited him to 'eat his salt' - which is a great honour. When Claude's first child was born (a girl - on 13th April 1910), they performed ceremonial dancing in honour of her birth, which they did not usually allow an infidel to witness. Great was the rejoicing - but it was the autumn of 1911 before Claude had leave to see his child.

In another letter, from Ras Dib, he wrote:

> I am Agent at Ras Dib and am in charge of 30 men. I have given up swearing because ordinary swearing is not powerful enough here. I believe they have struck oil at Gaysoon, this the picturesque islet I am off to some time in the future. It is our health resort, being cool and free from flies and sand. That is partly why I am going as Mr Wells thinks I have had enough of desert life for a while. I have had the toughest time of anyone here. I have the reputation of being 'made of leather, iron, wire and asbestos, otherwise would catch fire'. However the strain of the everlasting wind is telling, there is a continuous sand storm (more like a gravel storm) and the temperature is 120 degrees Fahrenheit. I cannot face it as I did. I am rather overworked, that is all.

Christmas day 1910 was spent in Jubal which Claude described as 'not a bad camp'. The men were chiefly Canadians and a jolly lot.

Claude spent a considerable time in Gaysoon. He wrote:

> It took 50 men a whole day to haul a boiler in place. I have 60 men under me and am as isolated and lonely as if there were none. I have a mixed lot of Bedouins from the Egyptian desert, others from Sinia and some from far off Arabia. The latter are a peculiar people - the scourge of south Syria and the bandits of north Arabia. They dye their robes a pale pink rose. Can you imagine a great brown, unkempt savage in pale pink robes! They stole 5

kilos of gunpowder last night - box and all. The government will not allow them to buy gunpowder and so they steal it. It is not so much the value of the gunpowder, but it being stolen that worries me. What with the Bedouins on land and the boatmen at sea, I never know what will be stolen next.

Muriel decided to return to Somerset for the birth of her first child. The little flat at Southwell House was still available and Muriel wanted the baby to be born at the little home she had shared with her beloved Claude. It was unusual for babies to be born in hospital in those days. Mrs Richards was delighted to have her and her sister Mabel, now a fully qualified nurse and midwife, was given special leave from the Bristol Royal Infirmary to be with her sister during confinement. Her brother Harry and cousin Maude were not far away at Bridgwater.

On 13th April 1910, Muriel gave birth to a girl named Ia Mary Adah. It was a difficult birth and necessitated the use of forceps, which left Muriel in a state of extreme exhaustion. The strain affected her eyesight and it was feared that her eyes would be permanently damaged. It was usual in those days to tightly bind a mother after childbirth to maintain her figure, and to keep her in bed for a month.

In spite of Muriel's exhaustion, there was overwhelming delight and rejoicing at the arrival of the first of the new generation. She was 'the wonder of the age' - never was there a baby like her! Congratulations poured in from all sides. A telegram was sent to the Tyacks at Church Street. Katy and Leonard were in the shop and called to Father, "Pa! It's a girl." Mother was at Enys Road spending the day with Leonard's wife. (He had married Ann Eddy of the beautiful hair and hands.) Both Katy and Leonard wanted to be the first with the glad news, and had a race down Wellington Road and then Enys Road. Katy caught on to Leonard's coat to prevent him getting there first, but he freed himself and rushed around to the side door. Katy, not to be beaten, called "Grandma" at the window.

A cable to Claude was carried by camel across the desert. His cousin - Muriel Bell, wrote from Skipton:

'Won't Claude be proud! He will be leapfrogging over the pyramids with joy!'

Claude's parents were also overjoyed at the birth of their first grandchild and after having four sons, his father was delighted that the child was a girl. Claude's mother was proud that the child was called 'Adah' after her, and made haste to find the family christening robe - two hundred years old and embroidered by Huguenots!

The ever-changing pattern of life, birth and death, joy followed by sorrow, spring by winter, the up-and-down swing of destiny, was soon to manifest itself.

Very early one morning, while Muriel was still recovering from the ordeal of her labour, her mother in Camborne suddenly started up in bed in great agitation. She shook her husband and said, "Charlie - I must go at once, one of the children is dying."

Her thoughts turned naturally to Muriel who was recovering from childbirth.

Charlie, rather annoyed at being woken from a deep sleep replied, "Don't be so silly, Lizzie - go back to sleep!"

But nothing would pacify her. She jumped out of bed, dressed in haste, and caught the first train out of Camborne station for Bristol, leaving instructions that a telegram should be sent to Mabel warning her of her arrival and to meet the train.

On arrival at Bristol, the story goes, Mother stopped dead on the platform and said, "It's too late, she has gone."

Mabel, in exasperation and rather annoyed at this sudden summons to Bristol, replied, "What is all this nonsense mother? Muriel is quite all right - I left her sitting up in bed."

At which Mother moaned "It must be George!"

George Tyack, at twenty-four, had qualified at Camborne School of Mines as a mining engineer. He was in his first post in Malay. George had a sunny, open-handed disposition, always caring for the more unfortunate of mankind. Claude had warned him that Malay was very unhealthy.

The chaplin wrote that there had been a very bad epidemic of blackwater fever. George, out of the goodness of his heart had volunteered to help with the nursing and had contracted the disease, from which he died. He had been buried in his dinner jacket. He had taken a turn for the worse at the time his mother jumped out of bed, and had died at the exact moment his mother had stepped on the platform at Bristol and said, "It's too late now." Before leaving for Malay, he had become engaged to a charming schoolteacher - Florence Brindle - who never recovered from the grief of his death.

In a letter dated 20th May 1910, Claude wrote to Muriel from Egypt, 'You have lost the "pick of the bunch".'

George's death was followed by a second loss - on 1st January 1911, Percy Sara died in California of a severe haemorrhage. Being an artist, he had lived a rather nomadic life, earning a living by fruit picking. He had been exposed in a storm and caught a chill which stirred up his old chest trouble. His father had dreamt of Percy covered with blood, being carried on a stretcher.

Claude was now the eldest son and felt it a great responsibility but it was late autumn before he could get leave to go home to comfort his parents and be introduced to his baby daughter. By Christmas, he was back in Egypt and spent the day in Cairo.

In July 1912 his contract with the African Prospecting Syndicate was up. In a strange way he had become quite fond of Egypt in spite of the sand storms and flies. The climate suited him and he had grown to like the Arabs. However, he was longing to see Muriel again and find out how baby Ia had grown. She was now walking and talking and he had missed so much.

Muriel rented a house in Beatrice Terrace, Hayle. Great was the joy of their reunion; but Ia was jealous of this strange man who took possession of her mother and called him "Naughty boy Claude".

8

RUSSIA

In 1913 Claude was offered a post in southern Russia by the Anglo Maikop Company, as inspector of oil wells, in charge of sixteen fields. Claude was delighted because at last it would be possible for Muriel to be with him. She was, however, pregnant with her second child and it was thought advisable for him to go first and for her to follow after the birth of the child.

Elizabeth Joan entered the world quietly in the early morning of May 6th. Mabel had once more obtained leave from the Bristol Royal Infirmary to be with her sister. She was so anxious that nothing should go wrong, that she summoned the doctor early, made a 'put-u-up' bed on the sofa, and would not let him go home until after the baby was born. She was a woman of great determination! The birth was easy and it was no world-shattering event as was the birth of Ia.

Two months later, Muriel set sail for Russia, on the *Imperatriza Alexandra* - St. Petersburg Express line, Riga Passenger Service, Russia, Germany and England. The crew were all Russian. Muriel looked very young and defenceless with a baby in her arms and a small child of three clinging to her skirts. The Captain - a great 'giant' of a man - offered her the state suite, usually reserved for royalty. He also appointed a stewardess for her sole use to look after her and the children, and to do their washing.

Claude met her at St. Petersburg and after spending a few days exploring this beautiful city, they took the long journey south to the Caucasus, first by train and then the last two or three days by road. Some days they would travel all day through one man's estate - they were so large. The further they travelled the more beautiful the country became. The sight of the Caucasian mountains took her breath away - it was so beautiful! She felt she was coming home - and before her was the scene she had often seen in her recurrent dreams. Muriel fell in love with Russia and its people - a love she never lost.

The Russian people took Muriel to their hearts - her warmth, gaiety and genuine interest in them, made her one of them. They admired her beauty and called her 'English Madonna'. A tall Russian peasant woman called Sasha was the children's devoted nurse.

Claude was away a good deal. His work took him to wild mountain areas. One day he stumbled into a village inhabited by the descendants of a remnant of the Crusaders who still maintained their mode of dress and lifestyle.

Claude always said that the labour laws in Russia at that time were in advance of the labour laws in England and each peasant had his own cottage and plot of land. One of the troubles was that corruption and bribery were rife amongst the officials who administrated the laws. It was even necessary to bribe the postman to deliver letters!

When Claude was on his travels, Muriel was frequently entertained by friends both English and Russian. Mr Penny, whom Claude had known in Tasmania, had been appointed manager of a nearby oil field. He had married and they had a small daughter Barbara - about the same age as Betty. Muriel and Mrs Penny became life-long friends. Mr Penny remained in Russia after the Sara family left. He was hung by his thumb from a tree for three days, but eventually escaped to England. He had a paralysed arm for the rest of his life.

Doctor and Mrs Ettinger became great friends. Doctor Ettinger was a Russian Jew exiled to the Caucasus. They entertained a number of people with strong anti-Zarist views and Muriel maintained that she had met Stalin at one of their dinner parties. In her innocence, Muriel did not understand the significance of their discussions but when she told Claude he was rather alarmed and told her to be extremely cautious.

Lewis, the third child, was born on 15th February 1915. Muriel rejoiced greatly at the birth of a son at last, delivered once again by her sister Mabel who had been given one year's leave from the Bristol Royal Infirmary. While in Russia, Mabel had many adventures. On one occasion, she saved a man's life by performing a tracheotomy (incision into the windpipe to create an artificial opening to prevent suffocation) single handed. She also nursed the wounded in St. Petersburg during the First World War.

In her 87th year Muriel recalled her memories of Russia in a little book, *Russia Remembered*, in which she gives a lively account of domestic life there, the simple peasants, their customs, and ending with the outbreak of war and escape to England. It is illustrated with photographs and drawings by her daughter. The following are extracts of her story from this book.

RUSSIA REMEMBERED

(i) Russia at Peace

As we were expecting our second child, I was unable to go to Russia with Claude, and waited until our baby was born. I had a little hammock made, which I could sling across my shoulders to carry our baby in, and reins to hold our little girl, aged three. She was just at that mischievous age when she was darting about everywhere. To complete my ensemble, I had a leather bag to carry across my shoulders, for nappies, pins, toiletries and all the 101 things necessary for a baby and small child and to meet emergencies.

I set off with every pocket bulging, my leather bag bursting at the seams, the baby in my arms and my little girl at my side. I had booked a first-class cabin with two bunks. In the morning the chief stewardess came into my cabin and said that the Captain wished to speak to me. He could only speak broken English, and I found it difficult to understand what he was trying to say to me. The stewardess could speak a little English, so, between them they managed to convey to me that the Captain would be honoured if I would accept the use of the State cabin for the rest of the voyage. I was very grateful, and most delighted to see it. The stewardess opened the door to reveal a large room divided into a luxurious bedroom with a very elaborate double-size bed. On one side a little single bed had been placed for our little girl and a charming cradle for the baby, and the other side led into a lovely drawing room, with a sofa, comfortable arm chairs, table, desk and bookcase full of interesting books.

I could not believe my eyes when I looked at the beauty and comfort of my suite; the stewardess told me that it was usually reserved for Royalty and that a Princess had travelled in it on their last journey, and I could well believe it.

My husband said he would be at St. Petersburg to meet me, and, wanting to give me every comfort, he had engaged and paid for a cabin de luxe to South Russia, which was more than a first-class, but of course he lost it and his money through our delay due to fog.

It was a joy to see him there on the quayside. He was able to obtain a room without any trouble at the Hotel de Europe, which was the biggest and best hotel in St. Petersburg. The entrance hall to the hotel was enormous, and in the centre stood a large stuffed bear, said to be the largest bear in the world - it looked almost alive and frightening. (A friend who stayed at the same hotel two or three years ago told me that it is still there.) We were taken up several storeys to a large room, half bedroom and half sitting-room where our meals were served. After we had settled the children, we sat in the window and talked and looked down at the big city below. It was summer, and I could have read the newspaper in the middle of the night without a light because of the midnight sun. As we had to wait nearly two days before my husband could get first-class tickets and a carriage to ourselves to go South, I wanted to explore some of the great city which Peter the Great had had built on a marsh, and sacrificed many lives in the building of it.

My husband did not want to go out, but I begged him to allow me to go, with the promise that I would take a card from the hotel to show the name if I lost my way. I set off to see as much as I possibly could. I spent most of the morning visiting the great Cathedral of St. Isaac and other wonderful churches, with which I was impressed. They seemed to tower above the ragged beggars who were sitting on the steps asking for a copeck - about a half-penny.

On entering the Cathedral, I was overawed by its wealth and magnificence - such a contrast to the poor scarecrows sitting on the steps outside. On the walls were Icons set in jewels, candlesticks of gilt and huge gates of silver set with jewels. Often from one of those lovely objects hung a cheap, tawdry item, such as a piece of hand-made crochet work or knitting. When a Russian received some special blessing, such as a new baby, or recovery from illness or something else for which they were thankful, they would come to church to say thank you and bring with them some gift. If they were rich, they might give an Icon or some jewel, and if they were poor they might bring some kind of work which they had made themselves - crochet, knitting or small wood carving. As the churches were looked upon as the homes of the people, they were allowed to place their gifts in the 'homes' just where they fancied.

I returned to the hotel almost drunk with all the beauty and wealth that I had seen. On hearing all about it, my husband felt that he would like to see the city too, so he hired a carriage and off we all set. We loved the great St. Isaac Cathedral where all the floors and walls were made of mosaic. Then we took a long drive out to the suburbs and marvelled at the wide, magnificent streets, lined on each side with mansions, beautiful gardens, and bridges across the river.

When we did go to the station for our train, I thought that the driver had left us by mistake at a church instead of the railway station, for one side of the great entrance hall was lit by numerous candles before a great Icon; a huge picture showing the Child Christ in the arms of the Holy Mother.

Many people knelt on the floor in prayer, rich and poor side by side. Later I learned that no Russian Christian would think of going on a journey without praying for a safe journey or a blessing on their visit, and they would repeat it on their return to give thanks for the safe return.

Our carriage was very luxurious. The Russian railway gauge is wider than ours, so it allows wider seats and enough space to set a table for a meal, which made it very comfortable for the week that we were to spend on it. Every night the stewards in white coats would come in with arms full of lovely fresh linen, turn the seats into beds, and every morning they came and took them away and returned them to seats. I did not see the necessity for clean linen every day.

One night I was awakened by a weird sound like the moaning of the wind. I got up and put my head out of the window to see what caused it. The train had stopped and there beside it were hundreds of figures in white garments chained together, their heads half shaved. The sounds came from the groans of the men and the rattle of their chains. They were prisoners on their way to Siberia, probably mostly political prisoners. Many of them were Jews because they had spoken out against some injustice. The sounds of their groans, the look of utter despair on their sad faces haunted me for a long time afterwards.

Some days we would be travelling all day through one man's estate; they were so large. The many onion-shaped domes of the churches were very picturesque, mostly blue, with golden spires which shone in the sun.

At last we arrived at the place where the railway ended, and we had to do the last two or three days' journey by road, putting up at the rest houses at night, changing our horses. The farther we travelled towards the Caucasus the more beautiful the country became, until it was like a beautiful garden, with lovely trees and flowers of all kinds growing wild.

The Caucasus themselves were a beautiful and impressive sight. The ancients called it a ring of mountains which encircled the earth like a wedding ring. The poets of the West called it a land of languages and miracles. For thousands of years the Caucasus have been the great dividing wall of Asia Minor from Europe and the home of the most interesting of all people - Christians, Mohammedans, Jews, pagans, and all kinds of ancient culture.

Our house was on the side of a hill, built of red brick, two storeys high, with large windows opening on to balconies all round the house upstairs and down. We had a magnificent view of the plains below. with the great Caucasus mountains at the back, always snow-capped. And sometimes, with a strong magnifying glass, we could see white polar bears roaming around. The bedrooms were large, with good windows and french doors leading on to the balconies. We had a bathroom with a stove in it, which supplied the bath with hot water quickly.

Then there was a small cozy drawing room known as the 'Cabinet' and all the rooms were well furnished. In the winter all the house was heated by Russian stoves, sometimes called Dutch stoves. One stove in a downstairs room would heat six rooms, three downstairs and three upstairs.

We had a good kitchen, with a large stove with several ovens.

The stove had a large flat top, and in poor houses it was often used in the winter as the family bed. When the fire went out a mattress was laid on the top and the whole family slept side by side on a warm bed which retained its heat for a long time.

Just a little beyond the back kitchen door there was a little stone-built house the size of a small modern bungalow which had two good-sized rooms. One was known as the bake house and the other as the laundry. Just a little distance from the house was a very pretty little house. When you opened the door you entered a little room with deep shelves all around. This was the ice house. The floor had a lid which, when lifted up, revealed a deep pit; in winter this pit was filled with snow which would turn into ice, so that all through the summer ice was available, the shelves were kept cool and food would be fresh for a very long time.

Before I arrived my husband had only engaged a cook and a boy, and he left me to choose the maid. When I was engaging a servant, or I had a Russian visitor, there was one question they would be sure to ask me - what was my husband's salary? At first I thought, why should I tell them? What business is it of theirs? Until I discovered that it was their business, for, if my husband received more than theirs, they would not attempt to entertain me as well as I entertained them. If we received less salary, they would not expect so much from us. If my husband received high wages our servants expected high wages, but if our wages were low then they would accept lower wages themselves.

My cook was a very religious Mohammedan. He was a wonderful cook and gave us many delicious dishes, but oh dear, when the bills arrived, they were enormous. As we could not then speak the language we used to leave all the shopping to him. We found out that not only did he pay top prices for everything, he paid himself and also the shopkeeper a good percentage on everything that he bought, which doubled our bills, so I knew that I must learn the language and do my own shopping, plus engage a less extravagant cook.

I loved all the seasons in Russia, for they all had some special beauty. In winter we had comfort in our warm houses with double windows. I have known a Christmas Day when we sat out of doors in the sun, in thin white silk blouses, and the children played and sat on the hard, deep, dry snow.

Claude and I, like two children, loved to go walking with long sticks through the forest of trees, white with ice and snow. We hit the hanging icicles with our sticks, and they would fall with a tinkling sound. All the world seemed white and we might be snowed up for months on end. Then one morning we would look out of the window to a golden world of golden azaleas. One could scarcely walk without treading on cyclamen growing wild, and from the ground rose the sweet smell of herbs and flowers.

I found food very plentiful and cheap, the most expensive meats costing about 4½p per pound in English value. The Russians used much meat in their soups. We would buy chickens, ten or twenty at a time from the hill men, for about 6d each. We usually gave our guests one each, cooked in fresh butter. A goose or a turkey would be about 2/6d and butter about 6p a pound. I was very fond of buffalo butter which was a pretty pale green: eggs we bought by the hundred at less than ½d each. I sometimes bought a whole dead bear at a time, and what we could not eat then, we would pickle and use when needed, and cure the skins for floor mats.

Claude was always a very hard worker and spent much of his time surveying and making tests, and, with his knowledge of geology, he was convinced that the real source of the oil lay in a little distant spot from where they were drilling which was only producing a moderate amount of oil. He begged his chairman in London to allow him to buy it and get it worked, but they would not consent for a long time. Not only was it expensive, but several oil companies before had gone bankrupt in trying to get oil there, but Claude was convinced that the real source of the oil was there, but at a very much lower level. He was so sure in his belief, that he said if it did not prove to be as he predicted, he would give up geology. After more talks of waste of money from home, consent was given for him to buy the land and have it drilled.

At last drilling was started. Claude even told them the depth that the oil would be found, which was deeper than any other oil well. Drilling for oil is a long and expensive business. More machinery was brought and huts erected for the workers. A big reservoir was to be made to catch the oil, if it should happen to be a gusher or fountain, before they had time to put in the smaller casing.

All this my husband watched over very carefully like a fond mother over her baby. Often between sets of tennis, he would jump on his horse and bolt off to see that all was well. At night he tied his horse up to the balcony so that he could get up and dash off to the drilling.

We anxiously waited for the first sign of the oil sand which is the first indication of oil. One day when I was ill in bed, he rushed into my bedroom holding a handful of dripping dirty sand, which he pressed into my mouth and said, "What do you taste?" I tasted oil and spat it out, and he was very excited. He knew that he had reached or was about to reach his objective oil. Almost immediately he received a cable from London asking him to go to one of their other fields some day's journey away, as they were needing his advice.

He cabled back, 'Impossible to leave, well in a critical state.' A cable from Head Office again ordered him to go. Before going he gave orders to the drillers that, at the least sign of the flow of oil, to stop drilling, see that they had the reservoir ready to catch the oil if there was an overflow, then replace the large pipes or casing by smaller ones, so that it would be a small and steady flow and no oil to be wasted.

One sunny afternoon I was sitting in my window writing to my mother in Cornwall when it grew darker and darker and everything seemed misty and my eyes began to smart. Whatever had happened? The telephone rang; it was to tell me that the well had blown a gusher, and this was about 2½ miles from our home. For days our house was sprinkled with oil. Cossack soldiers were sent for, to see that no one near would light a fire, lamp or strike a match to light a cigarette which had already caused a nearby forest to burst into flames.

The reservoir was not ready, so that more than a million gallons of oil in one day flew into the air and was wasted, and on top of that, we had to pay £100,000 or more as compensation for the damage to the forest. Claude returning from his visit and still many miles away, saw in the distance the great pillar of smoke from the burning forest. Glad as Claude was that the well had blown at precisely the depth at which he had said, it almost broke his heart that so much oil was wasted and so much money had to be spent on the forest. Had he been at home millions of pounds could have been saved, but in spite of this, it became a very rich oil field.

One evening my sister, Kate, in Camborne, went to the G.W.R. Station for something, and whilst she was there the train from London and Plymouth arrived bringing the evening newspaper. The paper boy who was there started shouting the big news - "A tremendous oil well discovered in South Russia! One of the world's biggest!" Kate wondered if it could be the well that I had written about so often, and it was. It was the oil chosen for the lighthouses because of its high quality.

I found the Russians very religious and they brought their religion into many things which they did in their daily lives. Nearly everyone had Icons placed about opposite the front door with lighted candles and flowers before them so that, on seeing the Icons on opening the door, they took off their hats and knelt before them.

Russians love their churches and seldom have I gone into a church unless I found someone praying or doing some work for the church. The two great festivals are the keeping of Christmas and Easter. I was delighted to find that the national cake was saffron, like our own in Cornwall, but made differently. My cook asked me for 125 eggs for these festival cakes. I thought I was being generous when I gave her 100, but later on when I knew more about it, I let her have the 125. The mixture is usually put to rise overnight. When it had risen, many tins were filled.

For the grown-ups, it would be a large tin - the kind that sweets are often kept in, and for the children it would be a cocoa or coffee tin, and a tiny tin for the baby. When the cake was cooked, it was put to stand on end, iced, and the top decorated with multi-coloured hundreds and thousands.

The cakes were put in front of everyone at every meal. The very best cake was kept for Papa the Priest, to be taken by them to the church for the Great Easter Service, and after the Service the Priest would visit the homes of his people to bless them and their Feasts. Nothing would be eaten until the Priest arrived, when the doors were thrown wide open with a great cry of welcome. He would say in Russian, "Christ has risen!" and all would answer, "He has risen indeed!" Then he would bless the food and all would be welcome to the feast, be he prince or beggar.

My servants kept Lent very strictly, eating very little; no meat, eggs or milk, and quite a few other things were not allowed. I used to watch them growing thinner and weaker and would beg them to eat a little more.

9

JOURNEY HOME

RUSSIA REMEMBERED

(ii) War in Russia

Just down below our house was the village green where the villagers collected on a summer evening to sing, dance and play. In the centre, dressed in their gay native costume, the dancers would swirl round and round, jumping high in the air, clapping in time with the rhythm and giving a magnificent performance. Never did the world look lovelier and more full of peace and joy as it did that Friday summer evening in August, 1914.

Before I was awake on Saturday, Sasha dashed into my room half-dressed, looking as white as a ghost, shouting the Russian word for 'War!' I thought she had gone mad. She said, "If you do not believe me, look out of the window and see, see!" I got up and looked out. Just below was our pay office and all around it were Cossack soldiers on horse-back and hundreds of our men who should have been at work in the oil fields. I dressed quickly, and went down to see what it all meant.

There before me was one of the most tragic scenes of my life. The men had gone to work at 7.00 am as usual, but they had scarcely taken up their jobs when the Cossack soldiers arrived, ordering them to drop their tools as they had to go and fight. They were not even allowed to go home to say good-bye to their families or to change their coats. They could only go to the pay office to collect the money due to them - the crying, the clinging and embracing, the wives wondering if they would ever see their husbands again. I went home and stood on my balcony, watching the soldiers driving the men away as if they were a herd of cattle, the women following and crying until the soldiers drove them back.

That was the start of the First World War, which came like a thief in the night. My husband was still away, so for days I did not know if we were among friends or foes. Only one man returned alive out of all those men who went away that day, and he was my washerwoman's husband, and he suffered terrible hardships in a prison camp in Turkey. The following day the soldiers came and took away all our horses except the very old, blind or lame. England mobilised on 14th August - two days after Russia. That awful war changed Russia and the world, with suffering, poverty and famine.

One night, Mabel was awakened by loud rapping at her window. She got up, unbolted the shutters and looked out. A very wild-looking man stood facing her. "Are you Mrs Sara's sister?" he said.

"Yes," she replied.

"A woman has died. Will you come and see what you can do for her?"

Mabel did not know what she could do if the woman was dead, but, anyway, she felt that she should go, and hastily put on some clothes. Not wanting to disturb me, she went out the back way where she saw some boots on the shelf. As the ground was deep in snow, she put them on, and followed the strange man into the darkness. He led her to a small house, where a woman was lying in agony on the floor, unable to give birth to her baby. Mabel concluded that the woman and baby would not live unless an immediate operation was performed. As there was no doctor available, she had to do it alone. She ushered all the people out of the room, and with the minimum of light and instruments, she managed to save the lives of the mother and the child.

Every day she went to the woman, and her surgical and medical skill became so well-known that she was in much demand and greatly loved. Sometimes the peasants would kiss her feet.

Our baby was born on a bitterly cold February day when the world was clothed in a black frost, we were in the midst of a war with suffering and tragedy all round us, 20 people dying every day from smallpox, and our own doctor's son dying of spotted fever. Before the doctor could enter my room, he had to have a bath of very strong disinfectant and a fresh change of clothes.

The baby had not been born more than two hours before Sasha came dressed ready to go out. She said that she had come to take the baby to her church to be baptised. It meant her walking with him across two or three miles of plains and on just the sort of day that wolves might be around. Of course I said, "No" and, knowing what a long and elaborate service it was, I said, "We will wait until our English Chaplain comes," although he could only visit us once or twice a year. She must have thought me a very bad Christian, as Russians made it their first duty to have their babies baptised, confirmed and receive their first Communion almost immediately after birth.

After waiting some months, the Chaplain came. We had fixed up one of the rooms to look a little like a church. Sasha was present and when in the midst of the service she burst out crying, I thought she was taken ill and went to her and said, "What is the matter?"

"Your Papa Priest does not know how to baptise," she said. "Please let me take him to my Papa who will do him properly."

The Chaplain also gave us and our friends the Holy Communion. As no wine was available, water was used. Claude and I sorely missed more religious services.

Claude did what he could, for he was a religious man; he could not marry people or give Holy Communion, but had long believed that working priests could be of great service in such places and could give their service free, for love of God and their fellow men, when necessary, and still continue their work or profession.

Mabel left for home after our son's birth, and before leaving she had received a letter from Sir George Buchanan who was the English Ambassador at St. Petersburg, requesting an interview on her way through. He gave her to understand that they might want her to remain there to help Lady Georgina run her English hospital.

"However much they want and need me," Mabel said, "I shall not stay; my duty is in England."

Some days after she had left, I was delighted to get a letter from her saying that she had to stay. Mabel had her appointment with Lady Georgina who told her how badly she needed a highly trained English nurse to help her run her English Hospital for which she had taken over a high-class girls' school. For hours Lady Georgina used every argument possible to keep her, but nothing she said would persuade Mabel to stay. At last in desperation, Lady Georgina took up the telephone and said to Sir George, who was at the Embassy, "Will you speak to this woman; I can do nothing with her." He said to Mabel, "As your King's representative in Russia, I command you to stay." She had no alternative, and I was glad.

Several Russian Princesses and Grand Duchesses had offered to help, but their idea of nursing seemed to be sitting on the soiled beds smoking cigarettes. Mabel said, "If you make me stay, you will have to do what I tell you." And she made them do the kind of things that she had to do as a probationer. She won their love and received several invitations to visit them after the war, which however was not to be.

Fortunately, Mabel had learned to speak Russian fairly well when she was with us, but it is not an easy language to speak. St. Petersburg is very unhealthy, being built by Peter the Great on a marsh. They were nursing under great difficulties, being short of supplies and they sometimes had to operate without chloroform. There were more patients than beds, and sometimes when the wounded soldiers were brought in, they had to be laid on the marble floor of the entrance hall until someone vacated a bed.

The Czarina often used to visit them and Mabel saw quite a bit of her. Rasputin also used to visit the hospital. One day he arrived just as they were about to have a meal. He said that he would say Grace - quite a long one - for which he expected them all to stand. One of the soldiers had a very badly wounded shoulder and Mabel told him that he must not stand. Rasputin ordered the man to stand, at which Mabel repeated that he was not fit to stand. Still he ordered it, whereupon Mabel told him not to interfere with her patients and nearly threw him out in anger. Things became so bad in Russia that the hospital had to be closed.

I have written before how kind our doctor and his wife Anna were to me. When Claude was away they would ask me to join them at meals and always when they had some special guests. Although they had no passport and were not allowed to leave the oil fields, quite important people used to come and visit them from long distances. I could then understand Russian and I noted how much their conversation was on 'change' - a change for which they must work. I knew that many changes were needed in Russia, and that Leo, Anna and many of their friends, because they were Jews, were unjustly condemned and that injustice breeds the revolutionary spirit. Nevertheless, I was surprised at many things that I heard, and said so, telling them that I thought they were very disloyal to their Czar, and that we in England would never speak like that of our King. They replied that in England there was not a person like Rasputin who tried to rule the Czar and the government.

Once I was so angry at the things I heard that I got up from the table and said, "I refuse to stay with such disloyal people." Sometimes on Claude's return home, I would tell him of some of the things I had heard and the changes which they were planning. He would laugh and say, "Take no notice; you should know the Russians by now and how they like to talk."

Living conditions in Russia were getting worse and worse; every day seemed to bring news of some fresh tragedy and awful, unknown diseases seemed to appear. Our eldest little girl was very ill, and of course I contracted the illness as I nursed her. My husband found an empty cottage or hut in the forest and sent Sasha off there with little Betty dressed in her red hood and cloak, and our baby in her arms. I thought that I should never live to see them again. I can still see Sasha's great strong arms holding our baby and Betty holding her skirt as they all walked away, but it was a comfort to know that Sasha would fight for their lives if necessary. I lay for days between life and death, only conscious of someone coming and putting water to my lips. As we had no servants left, Claude got a man who was not fit for military service, to come and keep the fires going and keep an eye on us. We were both very weak after our recovery, and it was good when Sasha and the children finally arrived back again.

Most of the English men had already sent their wives and children home. For a long time Claude had been very anxious to send us home, and would have if I had not persuaded him to let us remain. My husband would often say to me, "I cannot understand you. Any other woman would drive her husband crazy to take her away." At last it was decided that we should all go.

So my husband went off to the nearest city to get our passports in order, but we were told there that our old passports were useless. We must have new ones, and there were endless forms to fill up, and of course, more money.

It was two or three days' journey away, and out of our way for home. He asked me to join him with the children and the luggage at a certain place. We were allowed only to take very little and no books or papers whatever. I valued my Bible which Miss Butler had given me as a wedding present, and which I had had with me at all times. I refused to leave it behind.

Claude set off to get the passports, but instead of our getting better we got worse, and were mostly not fit to take any journey, especially such a journey as we were faced with and in such weather. But I had promised Claude that I would meet him on a certain day, two or three days' journey away, which would save much time and expense, and most important, fulfil our desire to be home in time for Christmas. We were only allowed enough money to meet our travelling expenses, and we had no money in England, having withdrawn it and placed it in a Russian bank.

The day that I had promised Claude we would leave, the children were so ill, and there was no possible means of communication to let him know. I had no one to help me with the children or with the final packing as we had no servants left. I should have set off after an early breakfast to do the long journey over the plains in daylight.

Everything seemed against us. Had the snow remained we could have done it in a sledge, but a bit of a thaw had set in which broke up the snow into huge blocks floating in a lake of icy water. The few Englishmen left came to beg me not to attempt the journey as the road was impassable; I still insisted on going so as not to let Claude down, so they said more horses must be found, but that was not easy as we had very few horses left, and even they had something wrong with them or the army would have commandeered them.

At last we found more horses, but by this time afternoon had arrived, and the light had begun to fade before we finally set off. It was bitterly cold and our carriage was an open affair, no cover or protection. I had to balance myself on a wood and iron frame, padded with horsehair and covered with leather, holding the baby in my arms, and grabbing our two little girls to prevent them from sliding off, and I had to hold myself on to the seat as best I could. The condition of the roads was beyond description, and at times the snow would give way and we would find ourselves thrown on to the cold, wet blocks of ice. It was pitch dark, and we were nearly frozen stiff, with me often falling on the children. When I picked them up they were so cold and stunned that I did not know whether they were alive or dead. I had done the journey before, but only in daylight, in the summer, with Claude, and then it was dangerous.

After we had fallen off the carriage seat several times, the driver found some rope and roped us to the ironwork which was very painful, often with my feet and legs in frozen slush. It must have been in the early hours of the morning when we at last arrived, more dead than alive, at one of our oil company's rest houses. A soldier was in charge and he had little or no food to give us; he could only supply hot water, which was better than nothing and helped to cheer us up and get some warmth back into our bodies. My only thought was to get the children and myself to bed, feeling that I would never live to get up again. We must have slept many hours.

Claude had arrived at the place arranged. When there was no sign of us, he was worried to distraction. He realised more than I did how necessary it was to leave Russia and that every day increased our danger.

Off we went over more awful roads, and when at last we arrived at the railway, we had to wait hours for a train, cold and hungry. When we did get seats, we might suddenly be turned out several times a day or night, and have to seek lodgings, as the troops needed the train.

It was always a fight and a struggle to get food. Morning and evening the train would stop at a station where there was a buffet. We had a thermos flask which we tried to get filled with hot milk or soup, if we were lucky, but sometimes we got nothing. One fellow passenger, seeing our plight, stole some food, pushed it under my cape and told me to run for the train. We never had enough to satisfy our hunger, and I was always haunted by the fear of having to leave one or more little dead bodies by the wayside. For some days when we were travelling through the war zone, the blinds were kept drawn and armed soldiers marched up and down the corridors to see that we did not look out. We had hoped that when we got to St. Petersburg we could have gone to the Hotel de Europe where we had stayed before.

We arrived at St. Petersburg about 5.00 am and had a sledge to drive us to the hotel, but they could not take us in as they were full of Polish refugees. We drove around in that sledge for hours frozen stiff. There was famine in the city and the dead were lying in the streets unburied.

At last Claude said in desperation to the driver, "Take us anywhere out of this cold before we freeze." He drove up to a place which was just a common lodging house, divided into many apartments. We were shown up several stairs into a room with cheap furniture upholstered in red plush, very dirty and freezing cold. As we were almost freezing after our long drive seeking lodgings, we called for some heat but were told that no heat was available - no fuel could be bought. We then asked for a hot drink, but no methylated spirits could be bought, and in spite of more and more bribery we had no luck. When Claude told me to give her an extra big bribe, the landlady produced a medicine bottle with just a little methylated spirits in and with that we lit the samovar. That was the only hot drink we had in the freezing cold in St. Petersburg for two days.

There was no lock or key to our room and we did not like the look of the place, and we certainly did not want our small amount of money stolen. We decided to take it in turns to sleep and I was to take the first watch. When we went to bed the walls of the room were a light colour, and as I watched I noticed them turn brown and then into a moving mass. Then the bed quilt became a moving mass of brown and made the baby shriek. I woke Claude up. "Bugs," he said. The plague of Israel could not have been worse. Only daylight removed them. The baby got bug fever and became very ill and never ceased to cry for weeks, which was not surprising - his little body was red, swollen and septic.

After we escaped from the cold, hunger and nightmare of St. Petersburg where we had only a short time of daylight, we travelled through part of Finland which was in the midst of a civil war.

A woman came into our carriage crying bitterly. I asked her what the trouble was, and she said that her brothers had taken different sides and she feared that they might kill one another.

Sweden was like a glimpse of Heaven after all we had gone through, as Sweden was neutral. It looked very beautiful with its lovely buildings clothed in clean white snow. We were taken to quite a large hotel and as soon as the door was open one felt warmth and welcome.

At long last we reached the ship which looked a picture in its cloth of ice. The Captain came to me and said, "I must warn you, Madame, it is very likely that your husband will be taken prisoner of war by the Germans, as we are being held up by them on most voyages, and all men of military age taken off, but you and the children will be all right." That was no comfort to me. I would rather be taken with my husband.

I was down in the cabin with the children looking through the porthole at the world outside which glowed with a golden light. What could this light be? I was so curious that Claude took charge of the children whilst I went on deck to see. Never, never shall I forget the wonderful scene of glorious colour which faced me. The Northern Lights were in their full glory. The gold and heavenly colours reflected their beauty on the sea and turned the great icebergs into dazzling pillars of gold. Its beauty was out of this world.

It was very rough passing through the North Sea and it was a miracle that our ship was not held up or torpedoed, for on its next trip it was torpedoed and sunk. The conditions on the ship were rough but we got some warmth and food of a kind.

Little Betty became much worse with malaria and bronchitis. I had nothing with which to relieve the trouble, and she was unable to stand. Gradually her breathing became laboured and finally she went unconscious. I kept praying that she would not die until we reached England, where she would have a chance to survive, and how could I leave her little body anywhere else, after I had fought for it so long and under worse conditions.

On landing at Newcastle the night before Christmas Eve, Claude carried the baby as he was heavier than Betty; I rolled her up in a down quilt and somebody directed me to the ladies waiting room at the railway station. With my big bundle I stumbled to the table, dropped my precious bundle on it and collapsed to the floor.

I picked myself up, started slowly and fearfully to turn back the quilt. Every woman in the room was staring at me, and a woman in black came and stood by my side, curious to know what I held in my bundle. Betty lay still and white. The woman turned to the others watching, and said, "She has a child; she is dead." She looked as if dead, but because it was what I feared, I shouted, "She is not dead, she shall not die until we reach Cornwall."

"I will go and see if I can find a chemist shop," said the woman in black. She returned with smelling salts or something, but whatever it was, it seemed to bring life back. How grateful I was to her. I believe that she also fetched me a cup of tea. How kind people were. Claude had to telegraph his father for our train fare. We must have looked a wild sight - untidy and unkempt. Goodness knows how long it had been since we had washed.

After some time our train arrived. The platform was full of soldiers and sailors home on Christmas leave and we wondered if we would ever get a seat. Eventually we got one packed in with soldiers and they were really darlings to us. Several of them insisted on sitting on the floor to give us seats, and made such a pet of the children and shared their rations with us - how wonderful it was to hear English chatter and laughter again.

Most of them left us at Bristol and Plymouth. I had a strange, wonderful sense of relief and joy at being back again in our beloved Cornwall alive. At the sight of Carn Brea and the old mine stacks, I felt truly at home. What a welcome we received. Jane, our old maid, kept crying and saying, "You look awful, awful! Once you were beautiful, now you are awful!" My looks did not worry me; we were home - that was all that mattered.

10

WARTIME IN BRITAIN 1915-1918

Claude, Muriel, and their three children, arrived at the Tyacks' home in Camborne on Christmas Eve 1915. They were in a state of collapse and near starvation. It had been feared that little Betty would not survive the journey - Claude was carrying her well wrapped up in blankets, in his arms. Mrs Tyack took Muriel in her arms as if she could never let her go, murmuring again and again, "Thank God, thank God." Tears streamed down both their faces.

Hot food was provided but they were too exhausted to eat much and were soon tucked up warmly in bed, Katy singing softly to the babies as she undressed them and tucked them up. Her heart was overflowing with gladness to have them home again. The bedrooms were cozy with firelight and it was wonderful to be surrounded by love and to sleep in soft beds, clean and sweet smelling.

The next day was Christmas and what a joyful Christmas Day it was! Claude ordered a carriage and the family drove down to Hayle to have Christmas dinner with his family. Mrs Sara, who tried not to show her emotions, but could not prevent tears of joy coursing down her cheeks. How Ia had grown, Betty had only been a babe in arms when she had last seen her, and this was her first glimpse of her grandson Lewis!

On 28th December 1915, only four days after his return, Claude enlisted at The Drill Hall at Redruth. This, as well as the brewing danger in Russia, had been his reason for coming home. He volunteered for service in Egypt because he knew and understood the Arabs, could speak the language, and knew the desert.

Some of his maps were being used by the army, but due to some 'bungle' he was drafted to the Royal Air Force groundstaff as an examiner and tester of the aviation fuel used on the planes. Claude was very disappointed. He was then thirty-three. He was ordered to report to the Aeronautical Inspection Department, 13 Albermarle Street, London W, on Monday March 6th 1916.

For some months Muriel and the children remained with the family in Cornwall until Claude was able to rent a house for them.

Ia and Betty were bilingual - they spoke English to their parents but addressed the servants in Russian, which led to some difficulties.

Life in London at this time was difficult and drab - a far cry from the beauty of the Russian countryside, and although Muriel was never the complaining sort, she had a hard time 'making ends meet'. The weather was often extremely cold and fuel was scarce, so the children would be kept in bed for much of the day to keep warm and they could then light a small fire in the evenings when Father came home tired from his work.

One major problem was obtaining food. Many of the shop-keepers were reluctant to sell to other than their regular customers; and besides, Muriel did not fit in at first. It is not difficult to imagine the stir and probably the hostility she aroused as she toured the shops, desperate for food, in her bright red coat with its astrakhan collar, and matching fur bonnet. She was tall and slim with long dark hair (on which she could sit), dark luminous eyes, and a beautiful complexion. She had the bright cheeks and the cherry-red lips which so often go with tuberculosis. For the disease of her childhood had struck again as a result of the hardships of the journey from Russia and of wartime London.

The family did not see much of Father as he was busy at the Air Force Ministry all day. He would visit the nearby market late on Saturday to see what he could get cheaply from the stalls before they closed for Sunday.

On Sunday, if it was fine, they would go for a walk on the Common, Claude pushing the pram with Lewis at the top and Betty at the bottom, and Ia trailing along beside with Muriel.

Muriel had made friends with her next-door neighbour who had a young family about the same age, so they arranged to look after each other's children one day a week. One day, when it was Muriel's turn, they were getting very naughty, running from the back door through a side alley to the front, and ringing the front doorbell so that Muriel was constantly going to answer it. It was dusk when the front doorbell rang again. By this time she was quite exhausted and very cross. She opened the door angrily and shouted, "You naughty children!" - when, to her amazement she saw it was her sister Mabel, wearing her Queen Alexandra Nurses uniform, and in great distress.

Poor Mabel kept crying and saying, "What a welcome! How could you greet me so?" After Muriel had sat her by the fire and given her a cup of tea, Mabel calmed down enough to tell her story. She had been nursing aboard a troopship carrying wounded from France, when the ship was torpedoed. She escaped with her life, and made her way to London. As the family had recently moved, all she knew of the address was that it was at Southfields. She took an Underground train and on getting out at the station, asked a young boy if he knew of them. By a chance in a million he was the boy who delivered the newspapers and he was able to bring her to the very door. The children, quiet at last, sat wide-eyed listening to this strange story. Betty thought it must be wonderful to be a nurse.

Muriel became pregnant again. Conditions in London worsened and Claude's parents begged that Ia should be sent to them in Hayle. Later, Lewis was evacuated to Muriel's family in Camborne. Jane who had been in service with the Tyacks since before Muriel was born, came to stay with Muriel in London. What a comfort she was! She was plump with rosy cheeks and bright blue eyes, with her hair done in a 'bun' on top. She was bossy but she had a heart of gold and Betty loved her. Mrs Tyack had brought her home when she found her, a small child of twelve, breaking up stones at the head of a shaft at Dolcoath mine, and until her death she remained one of the family. Betty used to wrap Jane's grey shawl around a pillow and pretend it was her baby and that she was going to visit her dead husband's grave. (Presumably he had been killed in the war.)

One day Jane took Betty for an outing to visit some friends or relations. It was a lovely sunny day and they were enjoying themselves when, suddenly, German planes came over. It was the first daylight air-raid on London. After that, Betty became nervous of bright and sunny days for many years - they seemed to bring a sense of danger. When it was raining it seemed to be safe as people would say, “The Zeppelins won’t be coming over today”. The raids became worse and Claude built a kind of shelter in the passage with wire frames and mattresses - or Betty would hide under a table! On one occasion, Jane took her to a communal shelter, dashing across the road with the night sky lit up with flashing lights.

They all slept on the ground floor then. Betty had a little bed in the corner of the sitting-room, with a screen around it. In the evenings she had difficulty in getting to sleep in spite of the screen. Claude had obtained some scrap pieces of wood with which he was making a cradle for the coming baby, and he also made a doll’s cradle for Betty.

Muriel’s labour started and she set off on her own by Underground for the Nursing Home where a bed had been reserved for her. All her other children had been delivered at home by her sister - Mabel. She had to change at Baker Street station and found that all trains had been stopped as an air-raid was in progress! She was afraid the baby would be born on the platform, but just managed to get to her destination in time. She gave birth to her fourth child - a daughter - on 7th October 1917. Everything looked so utterly hopeless that they decided to call her Nadezhda, which means ‘hope’ in Russian, and is affectionately shortened to Nadia.

The day Muriel was coming home with the baby was very exciting. Jane was making pasties in the kitchen and Betty begged to be allowed to make one for the baby. She was very astonished and disappointed to find baby could not eat it and, in fact, had no teeth! She asked to carry her round the room, but had to sit down very soon.

Eventually, as conditions in London worsened, it was decided that Betty should be sent to Camborne to join Lewis at the Tyacks’ home. It was a very sad parting. Betty loved London and the new baby, she adored her mother and loved her father although she was a little in awe of him, and Jane was warm and comfortable. She was put on the train at Paddington in charge of the guard and a kind lady who was a stranger to her. It was a great ordeal for a child of four, but she sat silently and did not cry. At the last minute, her father dashed on to the platform, having managed to get time off from the Air Ministry. He brought her an apple and an orange - almost unobtainable in wartime London.

She held them in her hands, treasuring them, all the way to Cornwall! A mute, lonely little figure, she was keeping them as a present for Lewis - who did not appreciate the value of the gift.

Aunty Katy and Granny Tyack welcomed her warmly; but she was distressed to find that Lewis was calling Aunty Katy "Mummy" and she said in disgust, "She is not your Mummy," which made Aunty Katy very annoyed as being unmarried and childless, she enjoyed the title of "Mummy" very much.

A few months later, Muriel arrived in Camborne with baby Nadia. Unlike the other children who were dark, she had golden curls and blue eyes - a cheerful jolly baby who looked out on the world bright-eyed and confident. A ray of sunshine in those dark days.

Claude was demobilised on the 4th December 1918, but remained on the Air Force Reserve. He was offered a government job in bacteriological research, which he would have enjoyed very much but declined because the doctors had advised him to take Muriel, who was still suffering from tuberculosis, to a warm climate.

11

MABEL AND HARRY TYACK

Sister Mabel Tyack was on her way back to England. The snow was thick and the train kept stopping and starting. The blinds had to be drawn so they could not see the country through which they were passing. Mabel was plump and pleasant with light brown hair and bright blue eyes. Miss St. Clair, sitting opposite, was in a terrible state of nerves. She had been put in Sister Mabel's charge by Sir George Buchanan - the British Ambassador in Petrograd. Poor thing, she had been a reporter in Poland when she was arrested as a spy. She managed to escape to Russia and sought the protection of Sir George who arranged for her to travel in Mabel's care, back to England.

The year was 1915. Mabel thought of England and of Bristol where she had been Theatre Sister at the Royal Infirmary, then she had leave to come to Russia for a wonderful holiday when war broke out and everything had changed. For months she had been trying to get back to England to join the Queen Alexandra Nursing Service for which she had volunteered before leaving England, but Sir George had commandeered her service to help his wife - Lady Georgina- to run a hospital for wounded soldiers in a converted school on the Novisky Prospect in Petrograd. What a time it had been! They had nursed Russian and German soldiers. The Tsarina and Princesses had visited the hospital. The Tsarina looked very tired and sad, the Princesses were charming, but Rasputin was the evil one - he had the most awful eyes. She had chased him out of the hospital once, when he tried to make a wounded soldier stand up for 'Grace'. She wondered what

England was like. She had been told that the Germans had destroyed England!

They had to change trains at Haparanda where an exchange was taking place - 200 Russian soldiers, wounded in Germany - for 200 German soldiers. The Russian wounded were like skeletons, lying on stretchers with perhaps an old coat over them to protect them from the bitter cold. There was no one to look after them. Mabel was so saddened that she was prepared to return to Petrograd with them when she felt a strong hand on her shoulder and a tall young man said, "No you don't." He said he would tell them his experience when they got into the other train. Taking her firmly by the elbow, he marched her across a bridge with Miss St. Clair trailing behind. On the other side there were 200 German soldiers singing and walking around in perfect health after the good nursing they had received in Russia - such a contrast to the poor Russian 'skeletons'.

So . . . after Mabel and Miss St. Clair were settled in their new compartment, the young man joined them. He introduced himself as Simon Hobson, an Australian. He said he had been brought up on a farm but had always wanted to be an airman. As a small boy he would borrow his mother's umbrella and jump off a hayrick. In the end, his father said to him, "Son - you had better go to England and learn to fly." So off he went to England and obtained his 'wings'. One day he read in a paper that they wanted airmen in Russia to teach flying, so he applied and was accepted. The English and Russians were on good terms then. His friends gave him a great 'send-off' and all went well until he reached Petrograd where an ignorant official, on asking his nationality, mistook 'Australian' for 'Austrian' and he was taken as an enemy. He was thrown into the terrible Peter and Paul prison which lies under the river Neva, without trial. It was cold and dank, the walls were covered with mould and were running with water. His clothes were taken from him. He was given black bread to eat, but could only eat the outside as it was green in the middle. The guards brought him boiling water to drink and tried to force it down his throat while it was still scalding hot. They leered at him and taunted him. After about 10 days of this treatment, he became delirious and was clawing at the walls. One day an official passing his cell, heard him babbling in English. An enquiry was made and it was found that a mistake had been made as to his nationality, and he was released.

So Mabel and Miss St. Clair travelled on. There had been so many examinations of papers and searching, and with each one Miss St. Clair became more and more agitated and nervous. It was like heaven when they eventually reached Sweden and Norway. Everywhere was so clean and bright and the people so kind and friendly. They saw Stockholm and Christiana (now Oslo) and eventually reached Bergen where they boarded a ship for Newcastle. They were told that Kerensky was on board on his way to see Kitchener.

During the night, the boat was stopped and there was quite a panic, all bags opened while a search was carried out for official papers. As the ship approached Newcastle, a thick fog descended. The first thing that Mabel saw through the fog was an English policeman standing on the dock. What a wonderfully reassuring sight! The tears ran down her cheeks. She was in England . . . she was home!

On returning to England,, Mabel reported at once to the Bristol Royal Infirmary where she joined the newly formed Queen Alexandra Nurses, and was measured for a uniform. She was given leave of absence and went home to Cornwall; but was recalled after only 4 days - such was the pressure on the nursing services.

Mabel was drafted to the 11th Stationary Hospital in France for about a year and then transferred to the 12th Casualty Clearing Station near the 'front line' at Ypres. She recalls in her memoirs:

> We had some narrow escapes and the mustard gas was awful! Then we got bombed out. I went on a hospital ship - the *Princess Elizabeth* - the King of the Belgians ship manned by a Belgian crew. There were three Sisters and three English Medicals.

They were carrying wounded soldiers across the channel from Le Havre to Southampton. Later the route was changed from Boulogne to Dover which cut down the time factor considerably. Mabel was torpedoed twice. In 1917 the crossing became so dangerous that women were no longer allowed on the ships, which were painted grey. Mabel recalled "our lovely white ships with the Red Cross, painted on them, turned grey."

She went back to a Casualty Clearing Station and was then ordered to Italy. This entailed a four day journey by ambulance, after which they were to travel by train. There were two Sisters, the driver, and their personal luggage. The ambulance had to travel in the dark, by night. They were held up at the Somme and missed the train with their food rations and equipment on board, and had to wait for another special train, so they were without food or drink.

At Genoa they were welcomed by a band, flags flying, and people clapping; but were weak and delirious from lack of food. From Genoa she was drafted to the frontier up in the mountains. Mabel was working as Theatre Sister in a tent from 6 am to 2 am the next day and sometimes around the clock. Anaesthetics were in short supply, gangrene was appalling, the stench almost unbearable, and so many leg amputations which each took an hour. One of the problems was that the skin flaps kept getting in the way and impeding the speed of the operation. Many of the men were dying of shock during the operation.

During a short respite when Mabel was lying down too tired to undress, she suddenly thought that if a soldier's tin plate was cut up the centre it could be used to hold the skin flaps back. She got up immediately and found a soldier and told him what to do. After sterilisation, it proved to be very successful and cut down the rate of amputation from one hour to twenty minutes, thereby saving many lives. They called it 'The Tyacks' Tin Plate Method'. A retractor of that design is still used today, but Sister Mabel Tyack who first thought of it, has long been forgotten. When her brother Harry was seriously wounded in France and required leg amputation, she begged to be allowed to go to him but was told that she could not be spared. He died of shock during the operation. They were so busy that they did not realise the war was over until two days after it had ceased . . . and then followed the awful influenza which was pandemic and claimed thousands of lives.

Harry joined the Duke of Cornwall's Light Infantry and was made a Captain. He was a man of peace who did not like to kill a fly. He wrote to Muriel before leaving for France, that he had volunteered because this was a war to end all wars and would make the world safe for her and her children. He was willing to give up his life if necessary, and if this happened she was not to grieve on any account or wear black, but to pray for his soul and for his men.

One of his last acts before going overseas, was to visit the beautiful little church at Penpons near Camborne to commend himself to God and to talk to his friend - Father Carah. Harry arranged for a beautifully embossed golden door to be fitted to the Aumbry or Tabernacle - a niche set into the wall near the Altar, which held the Reserved Sacrament. On the inside of the door the names of the men in his command who were killed in the war were to be engraved. He wished the name of the donor to remain a secret. It was only after his death that Father Carah told the family who had been the donor of the beautiful door and put the name 'Captain Henry Richard Tyack' at the top of the list.

Harry was badly wounded in France and thought to be dead. It was then discovered that a flicker of life remained and when he was well enough to travel, he was transferred to a hospital in London where he remained for many months. It was found that shrapnel had penetrated his chest, destroying three ribs and one of his lungs - in fact a large piece of woollen vest was removed from the cavity. On leaving the hospital, he was given a certificate stating that he was unfit for further military service, but instead of presenting it to the army authorities, he volunteered once more for active service, and returned to France.

In October 1918 he was severely wounded again. Muriel, who was staying at Camborne at the time, was in bed one night in a state between sleeping and waking, when she found herself in the midst of a terrible battle led by her brother. She saw the dreadful wounds inflicted on him - especially on his face. The next afternoon they received a telegram from the War Office, 'Captain Tyack wounded. Condition serious.' The Chaplain, when he wrote, described Harry's wounds which were exactly as Muriel had seen them! For days no hope was given for his recovery. A leg amputation was required. The family were all dreadfully upset and his mother beside herself with worry. Her sister - Mrs Downing came to stay and shared a bed with Muriel. Harry died during the operation. It was a fortnight before peace was declared.

Early that morning, between sleeping and waking, Muriel found herself once again in France with Harry. To quote her own description:

> I found myself in bed with my brother breathing in rhythm with him, the hard noisy breathing which some people make when they are dying. I believed myself to be dying beside him and then it stopped and I found myself back in my old room again. I woke my aunt and said, "Harry has gone." She replied, "How do you know?" and I said, "I have seen him."

They decided not to tell the rest of the family.

When they got down to breakfast, the family were all rejoicing because they had had a letter from the Chaplain saying that there was some hope for Harry. Three year old Lewis had found a flag and was waving it shouting, "Hip hip hooray, Uncle Harry is better." Muriel could not stand it knowing Harry was dead. She rushed upstairs to her room. The others said, "What's the matter with Muriel? They were so devoted," to which Auntie Downing replied, "Leave her alone." Some years later when Muriel was in Trinidad, she met a man who had been a soldier in the hospital where Harry died and he told her that the Captain, when he was dying, had a great wish that one of his family should be with him . . . so it seemed that his wish had been granted.

In the afternoon as the news was better and it was a lovely day, Mrs Tyack decided to have a country walk and visit her friend Mrs Paul, a farmer's wife, and to take Betty with her. The country looked especially beautiful, the sky was blue, the sun shone, and they had hope in their hearts. Mrs Paul gave them a warm welcome and a splendid tea of boiled eggs, splits and cream - a rare treat in wartime, but of course they were on a farm. On the way home, twilight was drawing in, and they were singing happy little children's hymns like 'Jesus wants me for a Sunbeam' and 'If I were a beautiful twinkling Star'. They were halfway along Church Street when Ia, aged eight, rushed out and said, "Uncle Harry is dead."

The shock and grief was too much for Mrs Tyack, she took it very badly, shut herself in her room, would not eat or see anyone, and kept moaning, "What have I done that God should take my beautiful sons?" She had had six sons and now had only two left.

Harry appeared to Muriel three times after his death. The first time she was sleeping in the back bedroom which had been the boys' room. It was at the end of a long passage and she heard and recognised his footsteps coming along the corridor. He came into the room and stood by her bed and asked her to get his Mother to stop grieving. He said, "I do not want to return, I have much work to do here and her grief is preventing me doing the work I should be doing." Then he left her and she got up, went to her mother and told her what had happened. Her mother believed her and gradually became her usual self again.

The second time he came, he kept saying, "Luu, Luu!" and Muriel thought he wanted her to find someone of that name. And the third time he stood by her bed and looked so happy and alive that she stretched out her hand to touch him but it was as if an electric shock went through her. She fainted, and when she came round he had gone. Although Muriel was a natural medium, she never sought the experience and thought it wrong and harmful - in fact extremely dangerous - only accepting these manifestations when they came.

The following is a copy of a spiritual letter written by Miss Botterell's hand (their old governess), and sent to Mrs Tyack three years after her son Captain Henry Tyack's death in France in the First World War. It was found among family papers over fifty years later.

3.11.21

Dear Mother,

I have been trying for some time to let you know that I am happy and alive, not to grieve and mourn for me dead and lost, for indeed I am not. It is a mistake people grieving in that way, if only they could see us as we pass over, they would think very differently. The passing is such a little affair when it is understood that is why we are so fearful of it.

Dear Mother, I have seen a great many here who have been able to let their friends know that they are alive. I have so longed to be able to do the same to you. To let you know that I often come in the home and that when you are sitting and thinking about me I am indeed very near. Not only me but George and Percy too, he has grown; he is no longer a little boy, he is a grown man; he knew me but I did not know him. Now we are three brothers here. I have also met Grandmother Tyack. She is not at all like what you remember her, she is much happier and brighter. George is such a good boy. It was comforting when I first met him. I did not quite realise it at first it seemed so strange to speak of me as dead then to find them all alive and moving about. Mother you must not doubt that it is Harry who is writing you this or rather giving it through Miss Botterell's hand you see I stick to the old name. She has given many messages I can tell you. Now dear Mother God bless you all and think of me as alive and moving around with you and taking an interest in you in all ways. George wants me to tell you that he has often been with you. Percy is sending his love to you.

Good-bye for the time. I will send again. Answer Miss Botterell won't you.

Love from us,
Harry

12

PEACE

It was 1919, the war was over, the promise of a land for heroes to live in had not materialised. The streets were full of unemployed, men on crutches - legless and armless in slings. There was the pathetic sight of ex-servicemen hawking tin trays of pins and matches, trying to make a pittance to keep their families from starvation. Widows were working long hours in factories or doing piece-work at home, or taking in washing in order to provide for fatherless children.

Claude was discharged from the Air Ministry, Muriel was in Camborne with the children staying with her parents. She had a recurrence of tuberculosis and Claude was desperately worried. The doctors advised him that the only hope for her survival was to take her to a warm climate and to leave the children behind in the care of their grandparents and Aunty Katy. He turned down a most interesting job offered to him by the government in bacteriological research and accepted a post as chief geologist and adviser to the Trinidad Central Oil Fields Limited, Tabaquite, Trinidad, British West Indies. As it was difficult to obtain a passage so soon after the war, it became necessary for Claude to travel on ahead, sailing on 14th May 1919, and for Muriel to follow on the next available passage.

It was heart-breaking to leave the children behind. Arrangements were made for the three elder children to attend Camborne Grammar School,which at that time, was fee-paying and had a kindergarten. Ia was nine, Betty six and Lewis only four. When it came time for Muriel to leave, she found it impossible to leave her baby behind and, against all advice and Claude's instructions, she took her with her.

The chief responsibility for care of the remaining children fell on Katy. It was a lot to expect of a young woman in her twenties. She was a wonderful foster mother and very much loved by the children, full of fun and a sense of adventure. However, care of three children interfered with her own chance of romance and marriage, as she took her responsibility very seriously - her devotion and sacrifice was taken for granted and not really appreciated. That was an age when one daughter, usually the youngest, was expected to stay at home and care for her parents and be a 'dog's body' to the rest of the family.

The Tyacks were Methodists - they had a sincere and living faith and although in many ways they were narrow-minded, their home was a place of love and happiness. They glowed with inner joy and serenity. They gave to the children a real personal love of Jesus.

Sunday was indeed a holy day. No ordinary books were read or toys played with; but in spite of the restrictions, it was a happy day. There was chapel in the morning when the minister gave a special address to the children, and special children's hymns were sung and there was the comfort of Aunty Katy's loving hand while little Lewis dozed on her knee. The Tyacks had their own pew - three quarters of the way down, on the left. There was the high pulpit on which the minister towered like a prophet of old, and above, in the gallery, a full choir sang heartily - red faced with effort. The ladies were in bright dresses or smart coats and fancy hats according to the weather, the gentlemen in their best black with starched shirts, and ties. Aunty Katy should have been one of that select company, but gave up the privilege to sit with the children. Somehow it was all so lively, cheerful, and cozy.

There would be a big Sunday lunch with a large round joint of beef, Yorkshire pudding, roast potatoes, and an assortment of vegetables. The beef would have been left in the oven while the family were in chapel. All the vegetables were prepared the night before and the large dining-room table set with a fresh white starched cloth and shining cutlery. All would stand and sing the Doxology - a hymn of praise and thanks to God - before the meal commenced. Grandpa, who hated waste, would not allow the children to leave the table while a scrap remained on their plate.

In the afternoon, Grandpa would sleep in the armchair in front of the dining-room fire, with a clean handkerchief over his face, which gently moved up and down when he snored. Lewis would creep quietly up behind him and pull the handkerchief off, which made Grandpa wake up with a start! Aunty Katy would take the children to Sunday School. She taught the seniors while Betty and Lewis would be with the infants. Sunday School was quite lively. There would be a simple Bible story after which the children made drawings to illustrate the story. Simple prayers were said and children's hymns sung, often with actions. There was a time when children could talk and give news from home, with special rejoicing and a cradle song to welcome a new baby in the family. After Sunday School, there might be a short walk and then home to tea.

In the evening, the children stayed home with Granny while Aunty attended evening service. The large family Bible and *Pilgrim's Progress* would be dragged out and the children would look at the rather horrifying pictures while Granny told them stories. When Aunty Katy returned she sometimes brought friends with her. They would talk to Granny and Aunty gathered the children around her at the piano while she played children's hymns. Each child had their own special hymn. Betty's was about baby Moses left in his basket in the bullrushes, which always made her cry, and Aunty would take her on her knee to comfort her. Lewis' favourite was about David and Goliath and he would strut about in a most warlike way. Promptly at eight, they would go upstairs to kneel at the bedside in the family ritual of prayers in which Claude and Muriel joined at the same time in faraway Trinidad. The ninety-first Psalm was always repeated and this brought a sense of family unity and God's loving protection over all - and so to bed, tired, happy, and secure.

Leonard Tyack, his wife Ann, and their three children, lived around the corner in Wellington Road. The cousins were constantly together. Enid had copper coloured hair, brown eyes and freckles - and she was only nine months younger than Ia. They went to school together and were great friends. Ia took the lead - she was a lively child, wilful and daring - who bossed and bullied Betty unmercifully. Joyce - fair haired and brown eyed with a wide laughing mouth, was the comedienne of the family. She was only one month younger than Lewis and they constantly got up to mischief together. One day, they both fell in a barrel of tar in the Tyacks' back yard. Fortunately, Aunty Katy, who had the job of cleaning them, took it as a great joke! Monica was still a baby and Beth not yet born.

To some extent, Betty was the odd one out but she did not notice it, as she was a dreamy child, who lived in her own little world of fantasy, where there were fairies and knights in shining armour. She was considered the ugly duckling of the family and she loved to dress up in pretty things, dance and sing softly to herself, and pretend that she was a beautiful princess. She adored Granny and loved to sit at her knee while they made up stories and poetry together, made pictures in the glowing embers of the fire and told each other little secrets. Aunty Katy too, was a great friend and champion against Ia's bullying.

After school the children would rush home and Granny would have some treat waiting for them like hot potato cake, dripping with butter, or home-made toffee which stuck to their teeth all gluey and scrumptious!

During the holidays, they would spend some time at their father's parents at Hayle. Here they played freely on the sandhills or towans - the Sara grandparents lived about a couple of miles out of Hayle at the site of the old dynamite factory. Grandpa had an office in the dynamite factory and they had a very nice detached house and garden which went with the job. When the factory closed, Claude bought the office block and had it made into a very nice bungalow for his parents with a room on the end as a playroom for the children. It also had a garden and an orchard. It was named Chy-an-Towan, which is Cornish for 'house on the sandhills'. On Sundays they went to church, walking into Hayle and back, to St. Elwyns church which was very 'high' church with incense and ritual. The service seemed endless and had none of the coziness of chapel. For the rest of the day the children were allowed to play as they liked. Although they had the freedom of the towans and playroom, Granny Sara was very strict with them. Ia was the apple of her eye, but Betty felt she could never reach her high standards, and felt at a disadvantage.

On sunny days, Granny Sara's friend - Mrs Garland and her daughter Frances, would call for them in her pony-drawn 'jingle'. Frances and Ia were about the same age and great friends. They would all crowd in the 'jingle' with much fun and laughter, and drive down to Gwithian beach with its golden sands, rocky pools, and fascinating caves. Each child had their own cave! At tea-time, there would be a wonderful picnic. Granny always made a huge apple pasty which was kept hot in a spotless white table napkin. When it was time to eat, it was split open lengthwise, covered with sugar and lashings of clotted cream, then closed again and cut into slices.

Sometimes, Great-Great-Aunt Fanny came to stay. She was Grandpa Sara's aunt but although only two years older than him, insisted on being called 'Aunt' - much to his annoyance and her amusement! She was the widow of a Methodist minister and lived in Newquay. She was very tiny and wore size 2 shoes, but in spite of her size, did wonderful wood-carving. Her other hobbies included exquisite embroidery and crochet. The children were fascinated by her. She adored animals, preferring them to children, and had a wonderful gift - any animal she spoke to followed her. If she talked to a cow or donkey over the hedge, it would follow her as far as it could go on the other side of the hedge - which made walks great fun. An afternoon jaunt was to Treeve Lane to turn the black beetles lying on their backs, the right way up with her walking stick. They could not turn themselves and if left lying on their backs, would die.

A particularly outstanding occasion was when the children watched, with bated breath, one of the tall chimneys on the dynamite factory being demolished. More excitement was offered when one of Grandpa Sara's pigs escaped and the whole family chased it wildly over the towans!

Buses were almost non-existent and when they first started, were thought to be rather a common form of transport. The nearest railway station to Chy-an-Towan was Gwinear Road station - a junction for Helston - and now closed, to and from which the children had many a hot and tiring walk. On rare occasions, there was a taxi. There were, however, few cars about and people were expected to 'use their legs'.

Aunty Katy had a pony and 'jingle'. A 'jingle' was a tub-like wooden structure with padded seats around the sides, and a door at the back, carried on two wheels. It was safer than the high 'traps' which were so easy to slip off. She would drive the children on outings to the north cliffs and sometimes as far as

Penzance to visit Mr and Mrs Ellery who kept a saddlers' shop at the top of Morrab Road. They were a childless but jovial pair and were ready with a warm welcome and huge cups of tea. It was wonderful to return by starlight, singing songs like 'Twinkle, twinkle little star'. Passengers had to get out and walk up the hills to spare the pony. There was no covering so one hoped for fine weather.

There were trams between Camborne and Redruth. Sometimes on a Saturday afternoon, in term-time, Grandpa Sara would arrive unexpectedly in Camborne and take the children for a special treat on a tram to Redruth to visit a toy shop and have a 'slap-up' tea. The trams were exciting with all their jingle and ringing of bells.

13

TRINIDAD

It was some months after Claude sailed for Trinidad before Muriel could get a passage. Muriel wrote in her memoirs how her condition worsened and she lay in bed tossing and turning. The time seemed endless. She held her side in pain when she coughed and her handkerchief was stained with blood. At night her clothes were drenched in sweat. She wondered if she would ever reach Trinidad and see Claude again. Thank God she was home in her own bed in Camborne with dear Mother and Katy, helped by Jane, to look after her, and she had employed Annie to look after the children. The children were loved and safe in their hands.

Then a letter came informing her, that due to a bad outbreak of typhoid in Trinidad, she would not be allowed to land unless she was immunised. Immunisation in those days was something new and not in general practice. She dragged herself out of bed.

Jane fussed all the time. "Newfangled ideas! It is all madness. And she has no right to be out of her warm bed!"

Muriel, feeling weak and shaky, managed to drag herself to her old friend Dr Tonkin's surgery. Dr Tonkin was aghast at her request and horrified at the possible risk to someone in Muriel's condition.

"Dear child," he said, "it would be madness to immunise someone in your state of health."

She pleaded with him, "If I stay in England I shall die, and you refuse! What can I do?"

He fussed and fumed but eventually said, "It is against my principles; but if you sign a form taking full responsibility I will send for the vaccine."

He came with it on a Saturday evening, in a very bad mood, annoyed with himself for giving his consent. After the injection Muriel fell into a drowsy state and felt as if she was floating on air. Her temperature fell to normal and her cough ceased. Dr Tonkin was amazed and wrote to *The Lancet* about it.

It was wonderful to feel well again and Muriel became very busy buying clothes for herself and baby Nadia. She bought several beautiful evening gowns, one in flame coloured chiffon, embroidered, and having a fringe of small silver beads. When she danced it floated out around her and the beads sparkled. She was indeed a creature of light and flame. Another was in a bluish grey smoky coloured chiffon exquisitely embroidered with flowers made of ribbon and seed pearls. She tried them on for the children to see and they clapped their hands and danced with glee to see their Mummy beautiful and well again.

At last notice came that the long awaited passage was available. There was a scurry of last minute packing and good-byes and Muriel set forth with baby Nadia in her arms. She had been unable to leave her baby behind, in spite of medical advice. It had been heartbreaking to leave the other three with their little arms clinging to her and their faces awash with tears.

A few days were spent in London with Claude's youngest brother Teddy, who was to see them safely on to the ship. He was recently ordained, and on the Bishop of London's staff, in charge of the Sunday School Institute. On the appointed day they set off early in the morning, but due to a half hour delay on the underground, when they arrived at Fenchurch Street station the boat train had already left and the only train available was a milk train stopping at every station. Muriel sat upright in a corner, speechless with anxiety, while she clung to the baby, who was jumping up and down with excitement. The journey seemed endless . . . would they ever get there? The chance of catching the ship grew more and more remote. She could have screamed as the cheerful station staff exchanged gossip with the engine driver in a leisurely way.

At last they arrived at the dockside to find the last tender had gone out and had returned. The ship was steamed up and leaving. Muriel was frantic. She prayed and pleaded with them to send out a signal to stop it. She hired a steamboat, and tying her broad brimmed hat firmly with a scarf, and clutching Nadia in her arms she stepped aboard. The sea was choppy and they were drenched with spray. The only way to get on to the ship was by climbing an iron ladder fixed to its side; but Muriel was not dismayed. She was a good climber due to much practice with her brothers, she had beaten them many a time, and she had a good head for heights. Holding the baby in one arm and with only one hand to hold on to the ladder, she fearlessly started the ascent.

It was a desperate climb with the wind howling around, and hampered by long wet skirts flapping around her legs and dragging her down, painfully step by step she climbed. Teddy watched in horror from the dockside. How would he ever explain to Claude that his wife and baby had drowned at sea when he was supposed to be in charge if them?

The passengers lent over the side of the deck, expecting them to fall into the sea at any moment. At last the top step was reached and kind hands reached out to drag Muriel, in a state of complete exhaustion, on to the deck. Nadia had enjoyed the whole episode, thinking it a great adventure. She cooed and smiled at everyone and went to their hearts.

Muriel did not know what had happened to her luggage, but to her joy and amazement, it turned up in another boat for which the Captain waited. It was a great relief to have her things although she had been prepared to take the journey in the clothes she stood up in as long as she reached her destination and Claude, her beloved Claude.

It was a very pleasant journey. The company had paid for a first class cabin with every comfort, and most of the day Muriel relaxed in a deck chair on deck. She enjoyed the excellent food provided. It was like heaven after the escape from Russia and life in war-torn London, and her health improved. Nadia was a happy, sunny child with golden curls and big blue eyes and everyone made a pet of her.

On arrival in Trinidad, Claude was at the dock at Port of Spain to meet them. He took Nadia in his arms as if he would never let her go again, nor did he if he could help it. She was his constant companion.

Before taking the long drive to the oil fields, Claude took them to Queen's Park hotel for tea. While waiting to be served three men left their rocking chairs on the balcony, to greet them. They

Nadia and Muriel Sara.

Lewis Sara, 1922.

Rock carvings in Venezuela.
Claude Sara on top of the ladder.

Venezuelan rock carvings.

Nadia Sara, aged 17.

Betty Sara (Elizabeth Flawn), aged 21.

St. Dennis Rectory.

Muriel Sara (left of wheel), with St. Dennis Red Cross
in the Second World War.

Queen Mary with nursing staff on the occasion of the opening of the new out patients' block for St. Mary's Hospital, Plaistow, at the end of the Second World War.
Betty Sara next to Mayor..

Nadia (née Sara) and Stanley Delbridge,
1946.

Elizabeth (née Betty Sara) and Alan Flawn,
1951.

Claude and Muriel Sara, February 26th 1966.
Their Diamond Wedding Anniversary.

were men from the Camborne School of Mines, who had been coached by Claude. They were constantly meeting old friends and Cornish folk.

The company had built them a beautiful airy bungalow. Claude had bought essential furniture, but left the rest for Muriel to buy when she arrived. The company supplied her with a generous blank cheque to spend in one of the furniture stores in Port of Spain. Claude had engaged one woman to work in the bungalow and a male chef. He left her to choose three other maids, two for housework and one for a personal maid. They also had a washer-woman. The first day she collected the clothes, the second day she put them into soak, the third day she laid them out on the grass and kept throwing buckets of water over them to bleach them. The fourth day she starched them, the fifth day she ironed them, and the sixth day she returned them. Everything was starched, including underclothes. Claude also had a manservant and there was Smith, the chauffeur, a great giant of a man who was Nadia's willing slave. In addition, they had two Indian women half a day a week to polish the floors with a special polish. Muriel thought the staff excessive but Claude said it was expected.

The bungalow was in a beautiful setting surrounded by palm trees. In the front there was a banana plantation owned by an African. Muriel asked if he would sell it to her and gave him the price he asked. A day or two later another African claimed part of it so he was paid what he asked for. Then a third claimed another part and was duly paid. Muriel also cultivated a plantation of pineapples, for which she became well known, by planting the heads of the pineapples they had eaten in a plot of ground outside the bungalow.

Trinidad seemed an earthly paradise to Muriel with its luscious plants, glorious flowers and rich variety of birds. The little humming birds delighted her with their brilliant colours. The following are extracts from a letter written to the children in Camborne, dated October 10th 1919:

> Last Tuesday we went to see a volcano named the 'Devil's Forest', it was very interesting and is still alive. Baby was so fascinated by it to see mud blown up and hear the noise. There was a little eruption there a month ago.

On Wednesday we got up at six, dressed in breeches and top boots, had coffee, got into the car and drove twenty miles. We got out and there waiting for us were six men and three hammocks, also two more of Daddy's men. I got in the hammock and they carried me four miles through dense virgin forest. It was truly wonderful. It was almost dark, I could hardly see any sky and was as excited as a little child at the wonderful things we saw. Daddy covered me with wonderful flowers and the natives amused at my excitement brought me interesting things to see and lovely fruit to eat. The birds made such noises. One bird made a noise like a great bell ringing, 'ding, ding, ding'. I love to hear the birds speaking to each other and the dear little humming birds, not much bigger than a huge bumble bee. There are so many monkeys in the forest. The native men like to kill them to eat as they think it makes them strong.

In some places the men had to cut their way through the forest. At last we came to the camp. I believe it is one of the finest oil crops in the world and the company has bought it and Daddy is the head geologist and in charge of the whole thing. The forest was so dense that I had to walk while two men cut down branches, as there were no paths or tracks. At last we got to the pit. I climbed down but could not stay because the gas was so strong. Daddy gave orders and off we went to see the wonderful crops, pools and streams of oil. You can see the gas fizzing out of the earth.

There was a wonderful breakfast waiting for us, salmon salad, tongue, native vegetables and avocado pears. Whilst we were eating breakfast, Motley was taken very ill, we thought he was going to die (he is the fireman). We did what we could for him and put him in one of the hammocks. He had to be carried four miles through the forest and another ten in Daddy's car to the nearest doctor and then another ten miles to Princetown!

On Saturday we entertained ten naval officers, who wanted to see the oil fields. We had a jolly time and they stuffed like schoolboys. I had prepared a lot of food and in spite of their appetites they could not taste half of it.

A visit to Pitch Lake was another great interest. The staff of the oil fields and those of Pitch Lake were on friendly terms and enjoyed many social occasions.

Claude and Muriel Sara's bungalow was open house to the young bachelors on the oil fields. They enjoyed the food and home atmosphere. Mr Duckham, the chairman of the company and oil magnet was very much at home with them. Muriel wrote to her mother on October 20th 1920:

> The only other bungalow Mr Duckham has ever been to is the manager's. He simply adores the baby and buys her sweets. He has bought her the best doll that could be bought in Trinidad. He says our bungalow is the cosiest and most homelike bungalow he has ever struck. He goes all over the place, even in the kitchen and talks to cook. We were told, before we came, that he was very much on his dignity and never went anywhere, more or less a little god.

There was a lot of social life in the oil fields, they were a friendly, fun loving crowd. On Saturday nights a dance was held in the clubhouse, but Claude and Muriel always left by midnight in observation of the Sabbath. Mr Penny who had been Claude's friend, first in Tasmania and then in Russia, was manager of a nearby oil field and a frequent visitor.

Muriel, who was always interested in people, became very involved with the natives and their problems, especially maternity care. She was elected to 'The Committee for the Welfare of Mothers and Babies for Trinidad and Tobago'. In Tobago the infant mortality was about 60%.

After trying a number of churches, they were introduced by Smith, their chauffeur, to the Reverend and Mrs Taitt. He was the vicar of five parishes and served a small shabby church near the oil fields. It was overflowing with a congregation made up of a mixture of Africans, Indians and Chinese, many of them walking many miles to church. The Taitts lived in great poverty in a dilapidated bungalow. The Saras made great friends with them, in fact Muriel and Mrs Taitt corresponded for the rest of their lives. Mrs Taitt was a delicate, pretty woman, who wrote charming poetry and was not suited to such a hard life. She was to lose her newborn infant on Christmas Day.

Muriel and Claude attended the church every Sunday and Claude was appointed church warden, but due to pressure of work he delegated most of the responsibility to Muriel. During the week, the church was used as a school for native children. The first thing Muriel did was to find another building for the school, and then to set to and clean the church which was very dirty. One morning Muriel set out early in her oldest clothes, with a car load of pails, brooms, scrubbing brushes and two of her maids. Their arrival caused much interest in the village and the natives flocked to help, the children running to fill up pails with water. Ceilings, walls and floors were scrubbed by willing hands. Next day they poured oil on the floor and wrapped the children's feet in clean rags. They had tremendous fun polishing the floor by sliding up and down it. Muriel made an altar frontal from two of her gowns, one dove coloured and one blue and embroidered with gold thread.

One day when Muriel was collecting money for restoration of the church and a new bungalow for the Taitts, a Hindu priest stopped her and presented her with a bag of money. When she explained the money was for a Christian church he replied, "We believe in helping anything that is good."

At Harvest Festival the natives filled the church with masses of fruit and vegetables, as well as more unusual gifts, including a goat. One African woman brought a hen which she insisted on putting on the top step of the chancel. During the most solemn part of the service it layed an egg, which slowly rolled from step to step, and before anyone could stop it, it broke at the bottom. At baptism, the women chose the oddest names for their children. One woman chose 'Umbrella', and Muriel, who often stood in as godmother, had great difficulty in getting her to change her mind.

The following is a letter written to Ia, Betty and Lewis by Muriel:

T.C. Oil Co.,
Tabaquite,
Trinidad.

18th September, 1920.

My Dearest Children,

Just a few lines darlings to tell you what a lovely time Daddy and Mummy had yesterday. We left on Wednesday afternoon and went to Port of Spain to stay at our house in Maraval Road. Did I tell you we had a town house? It is the guest house for the Co. where we can stay when we want to. Mr and Mrs Fletcher and ourselves occupied it for the Prince's visit. It has 10 rooms and is near Queen's Park so we can go there for our meals. We could easily walk but having the car, use it, thus we have three cars with us as the Fletchers' car came too, and one was used for the luggage. The ride to Port of Spain was wonderfully interesting, seeing the beautiful arches being made of palms, and native vegetables and fruits, and I saw the most wonderful sky effects I have ever seen. After arriving we dressed and went across to the Queen's Park hotel for dinner. It was most beautifully decorated with flags and lights. We sat on the balcony and met the biggest and richest people in Trinidad. Mr Ibbet was with us, you may have heard of him, he was specially presented to the Prince; well, we chatted, then had dinner, after which we went for a drive, then came back to the hotel and met some other people, talked and then went home to bed.

The following is Muriel's account of the visit of the Prince of Wales to Trinidad. September 17th, 1920:

We got up yesterday, had breakfast and put on our best bib and tucker. Daddy has a nice cream suit made here, and I put on one of my best dresses and hat and went down to the lighthouse jetty to meet the Prince of Wales. He arrived at 10.30 am. Then we watched him from our car inspect the Guard of Honour, ex-soldiers, and receive the Colours. It was a most magnificent sight. I would have given much for you all to have been there, the colours and plumes and the uniforms. There were hundreds and hundreds of men of all sorts in uniforms of all ranks and colours, white, brown and black. The Prince stood in front of us and shook hands with hundreds of ex-soldiers and officers. Mrs Fletcher teased me by begging me to hold my sunshade over him as he was standing full in the sun, so I offered her the sunshade to do it herself, but she declined. After shaking hands with the ex-soldiers, he got in the car and went off. Poor boy, he must have been hot and tired as he spoke to every man, asked where they fought, if they had wounds, and if they were better.

Then we went to breakfast at the hotel (our second breakfast, here they call it tea or coffee). We again met another big crowd, the chiefs of all the oil world in Trinidad, sat and drank limes and talked of what a nice boy the Prince is, and the men telling what he said to them, as most of them were ex-officers; several Majors who formed his Guard of Honour. We go and get breakfast and go back to the house in Maraval Road, as the Prince is to pass at 1.30. We have our house beautifully decorated with flags, Daddy and the chauffeur got up very early to do it. The latter got a big pole to hang our Cornish flag over the garden gate. We gave the Prince a cheer as he passed and hoped he would notice the flag. It was the only Cornish one in the island; then we rushed and got changed for the Governor and Lady Chanellor's reception at Government House at 4.30, as we had received invitations. I wore white satin with some beautiful old lace over it. I got nothing new but it looked all right, and a big picture hat to match, also trimmed with old lace. The sleeves of my dress were short and I wore the long white kid gloves I had in Russia. Daddy wore a new dark suit. Some of the dresses were wonderful, from Paris costing £100, but my lace was much admired. We were introduced to the Prince and shook hands with him, he's such a nice boy, a little shy, very sunburnt, and such lovely light, shiny golden hair. He wore a grey green check suit and brown sun helmet (in the morning he was in white uniform, we liked him in the white better). He spoke to Dickie Bennett after us, he lives in the next bungalow to ours on the oil fields, he is our doctor's son and such a nice boy. He brought down about 8 German aeroplanes. He has a scar on his face and the Prince stopped him and looked at the mark and said, "I hope you are better and did you get hurt anywhere else?" And Dickie said, "Yes, in the leg." That boy has a wonderful record, he is learning 'drilling for oil' now.

We had tea, ices and most wonderful things to eat and iced coffee. We stayed until 7 o'clock, then motored back to our house. It was another rush to change for the ball. I wore the white satin with the flame colour chiffon worked all over in silver tinsels and beads, the one I brought out with me. We went to the hotel for dinner and I wore a very effective flame colour evening cape as my sleeves are very short and the neck very low, nearly to the waist at the back, and yet it was too hot. Whilst having dinner on the balcony we watched the wonderful display of fireworks, and they came down in front of us. I wish you could have seen them. A specialist came with them from New York to put them off. After dinner we drove to the ball, it is a wonderful drive to the Prince's building where the ball was held.

Thousands of people of all colours came from all over the island to see the fireworks, and the Prince and all the people going to the ball. Only people going there were allowed to pass in cars and no one could go until they showed their card of invitation. It seemed like a dream to me that I should be the one going instead of amongst the crowd looking on as I have done in London. There had been a wonderful little lake made, covered with palms, where we got out of the car, then we walked up the steps and were met by the A.D.C., went to the cloakroom, left our cloaks and went to the ballroom. It was truly grand, hundreds of pounds had been spent on the floor and it was like glass. It was lit with hundreds, if not thousands of little lights, a throne for the Prince, the Governor and Lady Chanellor, and Major and Mrs Rust. Major Rust is acting as Major, they are dears. Major Rust often speaks of Cornwall to me as he knows it well, and Mrs is my dearest friend in Port of Spain. They tell me to look on their house as home, and I do and run in for breakfast, tea or dinner with them. Mrs is such a mother to me. The other morning I went to see her about something, and was going back to join Claude at breakfast, but they would not let me go and rang Claude to tell him. After breakfast she took me to her bedroom and got me into one of the beds and made me lie down, as she saw I was very tired, and I was really feeling overdone, so we both lay down and then tea was brought up to us and I felt very much better for the rest. He is an uncle to the Rust boy Mater met at the Berrys, very like King Edward, often taken for him. He is also a friend of King Edward.

Well, they didn't use the throne very much as I never saw the Prince sit down for a minute, he didn't turn up till nearly eleven. We all met him in the ballroom and sang 'God Save the King', then all the girls' hearts fluttered as they wondered which he would choose to dance with, but he had disappeared. No one could find him, he wasn't there, or in the supper room or balcony, but he had gone right out in the crowd amongst the Indians and all the other races, and spent a long time talking to all he could, and they gave him such a big cheer. He had won all their hearts, that made them his slaves, for they had waited for hours just for a sight of him never expecting that he would come and mix with them. When he came back he looked so tired, but such a brave, sweet smile, as if he was saying to himself, "I'm so tired, but I did it to show my love for my father and for his sake, so I do not mind being tired." I think little unexpected deeds like that do more for the King than anything.

Then there was a great, great cheer from the mob and we looked and discovered the lost Prince among the crowd. He came back and danced four dances, then went in to supper, but ate nothing, only had something to drink, and stayed 10 minutes, whether he wasn't hungry or was too tired to eat, I don't know. A most wonderful supper had been prepared, of all native animals, fish, fruit and vegetables. (Months ago when we were at the river estate we saw all the birds being fed for the great supper.) Soon after he left, the building almost shook with the cheers he got.

Well, I hope he slept well. He deserved it as he had had a most tiring day. He inspected all the people I told you about, visited the Council Chambers, reviewed, and gave another speech, opened buildings. motored 30 miles to visit about 7 villages, and came back to Government House to breakfast, then received the guests at the garden party, then to the Ball. The heat was great, and I am thankful the sun was not too fierce.

Betty darling, I wish you could have seen it all. Government House, a magnificent house standing in its own grounds, was simply covered in lights, done by a firm from New York. It looked like a glass palace glittering in the sun, so was the Princess's building. I do not know which was most wonderful, inside or outside, and under the house was like a fairy grove where we could sit and rest and get away from the glare of light and dresses, as most of the dresses were covered with tinsel or shiny stuff. Daddy said mine sparkled as much as any. The grounds had little native huts made of palm leaves, you would have loved them darling. I only danced four times. Oh dear! I was so tired! I just ached all over, but would not have missed it for anything. Daddy took a lot of photographs, I hope they will be all right, and Daddy and I were taken in the cinema film as we were about the first to be introduced, and we happened to be standing near the Prince. You must go to the cinema if they show it in 'Pathe'. I believe I walk in front of Daddy, who has a straw hat on and he carries a stick. I have a big hat covered in lace and my dress is draped in lace and I carry a fan, heart shaped. I face the camera first, then turn my back to it and shake hands with the Prince.

Sunday - We do not know if the Prince will be coming to our fields, on Friday night he looked so tired the Governor asked him if he would not like to rest all day Saturday after the strenuous day he had had, he answered, "Oh no! I've had quite an easy day, I would like some exercise tomorrow." So he went to the Pitch Lakes, saw Fernando and the oil fields near, but he says he wants to see the best oil in Trinidad. Ours is the best so I hope he will come.

I wanted to send you our ball invitation, but had to give it up.

The decorations of Port of Spain were indeed wonderful. Great arches made of thousands and thousands of mature fruits and nuts of marvellous colours. For months before, everyone had guarded everything special that they had in fruit, flowers and vegetables and goods to be kept for the royal visit, almost everything grown from here, with the hope that the Prince would see or taste it. How sad we were that he ate little or nothing of the tempting bounty that we had worked and saved for months.

These Royal tours must take a lot out of our Royal Family, and must cost a lot to prepare, but we who have seen and helped to prepare know only too well how worth while it all is and money well spent. How much it means to the natives to know that their Sovereign cares for them, comes to see them, hold out their hearts and hands in friendship, let them know that they belong to each other. To work for each with honour and good, it gives the family spirit. Before this visit things were not safe or compatible between the races. Afterwards we could go to anywhere in safety. He showed us, he in his high position, mixed and showed love and freedom to our coloured brothers and sisters showing us how we could show more friendship, sympathy and understanding to our coloured friends.

Nadia was a great favourite on the oil fields. She very much resented having to wear clothes when the black children wore nothing. So one day she got hold of the black shoe polish and brush, removed her clothes and proceeded to cover herself with black polish. On another occasion Muriel had gone to Port of Spain to do some shopping and left Nadia in the car in Smith's charge. He slipped off for a few minutes on some errand or other. When Muriel returned she found Nadia standing up in the back of the car stark naked and covering herself with flour, which she had found in a bag, and patting her tummy saying, "Pretty powder Mummy, pretty powder." She also had her own little table and dainty rosebud china for her own use when Muriel had a tea party. Muriel and Claude delighted in showering on her all the little pleasures they had had to deny the other children during the difficult war years.

On Saturday mornings Miss Genue would call at the oil fields at 7 am She was young, little more than a girl, tall, slim, beautiful, wearing the prettiest dresses and dainty high heeled shoes. But beneath this deceptive appearance lay a shrewd and gifted business woman. Her father had left Switzerland and settled in Trinidad. He bought a forest, built a saw mill, set up as a timber merchant hoping to make a fortune. Before he was able to recover his expenses he was killed in an accident, leaving a broken hearted wife and large family without money. His eldest daughter, aged only seventeen, left school and took over her father's business and family fortunes. She also contracted gangs of men out for work and had a large contract with the oilfields. Their home was built like a Swiss chalet, set in a beautiful garden and at the garden gate she built a smaller chalet and opened a small shop, which became very prosperous. As well as all these activities she became registrar for births, deaths and marriages.

She and Muriel became great friends, so on Saturdays she would arrive early to plan and superintend her men's work, then come to breakfast with the Saras and spend the morning with them. She was a wonderful sewing woman and would say, "have you any sewing I can do?" and would alter or make the most delightful dresses in next to no time, without charge, sometimes with a hat to match. The children loved her and their great delight was to ask her to take down her beautiful corn coloured hair, which was plaited and wound like a crown around her head. When loose, it fell to the ground and surrounded her like a beautiful golden cloak. At midday she would go to inspect her men's work and pay their wages and collect the money due to her.

It seemed strange to see this fair young girl in her silk stockings and high heeled shoes walking through all the filth and mud of the oil fields to inspect the work of a burly gang of black men, and the respect she received from them. She refused all offers of marriage saying "Mam and the children need me."

After two years Claude and Muriel returned to England for a short holiday and decided to take Lewis with them when they returned to Trinidad. Betty aged eight, pleaded to go with them, and Muriel took her to see Dr Tonkin for a medical examination. As Betty had suffered badly from malaria in Russia and had had an enlarged spleen, he advised strongly against it, much to her grief, malaria in such a young child being unusual. It was decided that Ia and Betty should go to boarding school, Thorneloe at Weymouth.

At this time Claude had made quite a name for himself in the oil world and was considered one of the foremost consultant geologists of his day. He was always a modest man and inclined to underrate his achievements. Hard working and honest to the highest degree, he preferred home life and family to all the social life of the camp on which Muriel thrived. As he was often away from home very hard at work with little time to spare and great responsibility, he was glad that she had so many friends and so much to interest her.

Lewis enjoyed life in Trinidad very much and soon became popular on the oil fields. The most exciting adventure of all was a visit to Robinson Crusoe's cave on the island of Tobago. He wanted to know where the cat had gone and the guide told him it had disappeared into the bush and gone wild.

Tobago, Robinson Crusoe's island, is considered the most beautiful of the West Indian islands. Muriel was asked to go there as a representative of the Maternity Infant Welfare Committee for Trinidad and Tobago in order to set up a welfare centre and midwifery service. She, Lewis and Nadia were invited to stay at the Fort at Scarborough as guests of Mr and Mrs Sonjano, a delightful couple with whom they spent a month, October 1922. Sonjano was warden of the island or acting Governor. The Fort was an enormous building with huge empty prisons underneath. Muriel used to imagine at night that she could hear the cries of the long dead prisoners. They spent a glorious month on this beautiful island and to the great joy of the children, visited Robinson Crusoe's cave.

During their stay in Trinidad, Nadia developed a severe attack of rheumatic fever which left her with a cardiac valvular disease, and this remained with her, although eventually it became well compensated.

In 1923, after four years in Trinidad, the Saras left for the last time and returned to Cornwall. After some months Claude went to Venezuela, leaving Muriel and the children in Cornwall.

14

THORNELOE

Thorneloe was a select private school for girls, run by two maiden ladies, Miss Bussel and Miss James. The senior Miss Bussel was tall, thin and severe looking. She wore a pince-nez. By contrast Miss James was short, plump and motherly. They were the best of friends, in spite of, or because of their differences. The school was housed in a large Victorian building in Rodney, a suburb of Weymouth.

Miss Bussel and Miss James were very careful in their selection of girls and only accepted those from the most select families. Ia and Betty were approved because their Uncle Teddy had been a curate in the town and a great favourite with the headmistresses. He had married Mary Butler, their classics mistress, whom he had met as a student in Dublin. Her father had been the university curator and she a fellow student.

Granny Sara had the responsibility of fitting the children out for school, as well as making and embroidering some of the garments herself. A seamstress came for a week to help, everything was beautifully done. Granny would not tolerate anything slapdash.

Thorneloe was a happy school. Its aim was not to train girls for a career or to earn their own living, but to teach them the social graces and to turn them out as cultured and well mannered young ladies. Many of them would go on to finishing school in France. After breakfast each morning they would return to their dormitory to manicure their nails. On every Saturday evening in the winter, a party was held and the girls wore white dresses and were taught to curtsy in real court fashion. This was followed by dancing such things as 'Richard-de-Coverly' or 'The Lancers'. Each child was expected to sing a song or give a recitation.

In the summer, weather permitting, the children were taken on a picnic. This was great fun and they were allowed to buy ginger beer in stone bottles.

Betty, as the baby of the boarders, was only eight, and was made something of a pet. She had a small bed in the assistant matron's room at the end of the junior dormitory which held 10 little girls. It was lonely to be in a room on her own away from the other girls and she was afraid of the dark. Margaret Appleyard, who had a kind heart, would sometimes sneak out and sit on the bed to comfort her. Miss James who loved the little ones, would sometimes put a few sweets under the infants' pillows and say the fairies had put them there - perhaps not very good for teeth, but a great comfort to homesick little girls. Ia who was eleven, slept in a more senior dormitory. She had made friends with girls her own age and could not be bothered with a timid little sister.

In the mornings the girls stripped to the waist to wash, and in Lent as a penance, they washed in ice cold water. In those days central heating was not common and in the winter the school seemed bitterly cold after the milder climate of Cornwall. Betty would excuse herself from class in order to go to the cloakroom and warm her hands under the hot water tap, which gave her the most awful chilblains. She was forced to eat fat which made her sick and so gained the reputation of having a weak stomach, and to her disgust at parties, was only allowed to eat jelly which she disliked.

The sick room was papered with enormous bunches of roses and grapes, the counting of which would almost send a sick child over the brink.

The focus of interest was the neighbouring boys prep school. On Sundays both schools attended the tin roofed mission church, the girls sitting on one side of the isle and the boys on the other. Many a sly glance passed between them. The two highlights were attendance at the boys' cricket match in the summer and their fancy dress dance at Christmas. Another great event was the production of *Midsummer Night's Dream* by the school and Betty was given the part of Ariel, clothed in chiffon handkerchiefs stitched together.

The holidays were divided between the Tyacks at Camborne and the Saras at Hayle. After two years, Claude and Muriel and the younger children returned from Trinidad. It was the Easter holiday, but Ia had to stay at school because she had chickenpox. Betty was put on the train at Weymouth, in charge of the guard. It was arranged that Muriel would meet her at Yeovil where she had to change. When she alighted at Yeovil, Muriel was on the platform walking up and down looking for her small daughter, and although Betty stood directly in front of her, she did not recognise this forlorn little figure in school uniform, with her face almost hidden by a hideous black beaver hat, until Betty caught hold of her skirt and said, "I am Betty."

When the dynamite factory closed, Grandpa Sara, encouraged by Father Berry, Vicar of St. Elwyn's, decided to apply for Ordination in the Church of England. He had for a number of years been a lay reader; because of his age he was allowed to do a course of study and take his examinations at home. The great day came! Ia and Betty accompanied Granny to Truro cathedral to see their grandfather ordained. It was an awe inspiring occasion for them. Their parents and the younger children were in Trinidad.

So in his sixties William Sara found his true vocation and was happier and more fulfilled than he had ever been. After his Ordination he took services on alternate Sundays at Gwithian and Phillack churches. Both were very old, going back to the dawn of Christianity in Britain. Phillack's origin is reputed to go back to the fifth century, Ia and Betty loved to walk to church with him through lanes riotous with wild flowers. On the way to Gwithian the hedges were so wide that there was a path on top, on which the girls found it great fun to walk, taking care not to spoil their Sunday clothes.

Later, Mr William Sara became Curate at Heamoor, in the Parish of Madron near Penzance. His duties included taking a monthly morning service at Morvah, a charming little candle lit church in a quiet village on the north coast, between St. Ives and Land's End.

Finally, William Sara became Vicar of St. Veep before retiring to Lostwithiel. The church and vicarage were set in the most glorious countryside above the Fowey river. The vicarage was very old and very beautiful.

15

1923

In September 1923 Claude sailed for Venezuela. It was a sad good-bye. Muriel, Ia and Betty accompanied him in a cab to Gwinear Road station. Ia and Betty stared fixedly out of the window trying not to cry. They had had Daddy home for the whole summer and it had been wonderful to have been a complete family again.

They had stayed with Granny and Grandpa Sara at Chy-an-Towan. Daddy had given them morning lessons in the playroom. He had been very strict. In the afternoons they had had glorious times on the beach, a wonderful stretch of sand between Hayle and Gwithian, which they had to themselves. When the tide was out it was half a mile wide and the sand was firm enough to play games on. The gold of the sands, the blue of the sea and sky were intoxicating and they could safely run in the nude, free as birds. Daddy was a wonderful swimmer and knew the currents and moods of the sea. Sometimes he would only let them get wet and come straight out again. They would roly-poly down the sand hills to dry themselves in the warm sand.

Daddy would read to them when they were in bed, Spenser's *Fairie Queene* in its original verse. He wanted them to love the classics and poetry as he did. Although they were so young, they revelled in the beauty of words and were transported to the land of fairies - and now the magic time was over.

They had run up and down on the gravel in Daddy's high jungle boots, to make them look worn so that he would not have to pay duty on new boots.

One day Ivy had arrived. Mummy had hired her to help with the children and housework. Granny always had Gladys, whom they loved dearly, but Ivy was to be their own. She arrived with the cabbages and carrots in her father's greengrocer's cart, straight from school, pretty and demure. With her long beech coloured hair done up in a bun, large blue eyes and rosy cheeks, she became at once one of them.

Clip clop went the horses' hooves as they passed through the winding lanes, the hedges rich with late summer flowers. Claude had never felt so desolate in his life. Gwinear Road station was set in the middle of the country, but the main line stopped there as it was a junction for Helston. There was a hustle and bustle as the trunk and baggage were transferred to the luggage van. There were hectic last minute hugs and kisses. The guard slammed the door, blew his whistle, waved his red flag and the train was off. The children ran along the platform waving frantically until the train was out of sight.

Muriel rented a house temporarily at Penpol Terrace, Hayle, while looking for suitable accommodation in Penzance. She found a pleasant, three storied terraced house eventually, at Greenbank, on the outskirts of the town. It was in easy walking distance for schools. It was arranged that Ia and Betty should attend the Church of England High School, later to become St. Clare's. Lewis was to attend St. Erbyn's Preparatory School for boys. Due to the strain of parting with Claude and setting up house, Muriel became ill and had to spend some weeks in bed. Ivy took over the management of the house and proved a treasure.

Muriel had intended to send Nadia to a small private school run by Miss Bell at Alverton Place. She was the sister of Aunt Fanny's husband, the Reverend Fred Bell, but due to her illness, no arrangements had been made. Nadia, aged six, became tired of waiting for Mummy to get better and decided to make her own arrangements. She dressed herself in her little green coat, leggings and tricorn hat, looking like a miniature Robin Hood, and skipped out of the house unnoticed. She rang the bell at the tall house and asked to speak to Miss Bell. Due to having spent most of her life in the West Indies, Nadia spoke in a high sing song voice with its own peculiar accent, which was difficult to understand. Miss Bell, tall, thin and elderly, looked down at this small green imp and could not understand a word she was saying. Eventually she managed to make out where she was living and arranged with one of the staff to take her home and find out what it was all about.

Ia was very happy at school, she was bright, good at games, self confident and a good mixer. Betty on the other hand was most unhappy there. The bigness and bustle of the school, with its hearty hockey-loving girls, frightened her. She longed for small, friendly Thorneloe. Shy and forlorn she retreated into writing poetry and day dreaming.

As Muriel's health improved she began to take an interest in local affairs, and her natural vivacity and love of life returned. She was an erratic and indifferent housekeeper, preferring social activity to domestic routine. She became a member of the Royal Geological Society and took a keen interest in politics and attended classes for making jewellery at the Art School. Due to her love of people she soon made friends and had a special care for the elderly and infirm.

Lady Ebury, who as Mary Glasson had been Muriel's school-girl friend, bought 'The Gew' at Marazion, and became Auntie Molly to the children. When she married Francis Grosvenor, he had been a third son and not expected to inherit the title. They had been very happy on their ranch in Canada; but both elder brothers were killed in the First World War and Francis inherited the title, much to Mary's dismay. She loved cooking and entertaining her friends, but had no taste for high society. On one occasion when Muriel was visiting her at Moor Park, the family estate, Mary was due to open a garden fête which she loathed doing. She persuaded Muriel to dress up in her clothes and impersonate her. No one noticed the difference. Muriel played the part with gusto and they both thought it hilarious.

So Mary decided to retire to Cornwall and renewed her friendship with Muriel and her family. She gave the most wonderful parties when 'sardines' were played all over the house. Her pasties and cakes were delicious. Betty never forgot the warmth and kindness she received from this generous lady. There was a special empathy between them. Her daughter, also called Betty, eighteen and very beautiful, spent most of her time in London, acting as hostess for her father. Billy, at fourteen, over six foot tall and resembling his famous ancestor, the Duke of Wellington, was at Harrow. Peter, the youngest, lived with his mother and was looked after by a nanny.

While living at Greenbank, Muriel became friendly with the two Misses Hope, who lived in a lovely old thatched cottage opposite. They had a Russian maid, Marie Chargin, tall, thin and middle-aged. She bore herself with great dignity, and had a pale, sad face. Muriel loved to talk to her and invited her to her home. They became the greatest of friends. Madam Chargin, as the children called her, came from one of the noblest families in Russia. Her father was a famous general and a great friend of the late Czar's father, with whom he had shared a nursery. She had been a Godchild and favourite of the Czar and a great court beauty. On occasions when the Czarina was indisposed, the Czar would choose her as his partner to open a state ball. He also sometimes sent her on secret missions which he could trust to no one else. Her uncle had been governor of Moscow. She married into the former ruling house of Crimea, a Baron Chargin, but preferred not to use her title.

When the revolution came they lost all their lands and she sold her jewellery to help the poor and needy. She nursed in a hospital, treating all with equal love and care. Because of her kindness she was helped to escape with her son in a ship crossing the Black Sea.

She never showed self pity or regret for her past life, from living in palaces to scrubbing floors and cleaning grates. All she would say was "Deary, it is all experience and:

"Life is a story in volumes three,
The past the present and the to be,
The past is finished and put away,
The present is what we are living day by day,
The third and last of the volumes three is hidden
From sight God has the key."

There was something rather strange about the Greenbank. If Muriel and Ivy were late going to bed, at midnight they would hear ghostly footsteps ascending the stairs and would cling to each other in terror. The children, who knew nothing of this, were fast asleep in bed. Muriel asked her neighbour if she heard the same footsteps.

"No," she replied, "but you know a double murder took place in your house." It was some time after this that Muriel decided to look for another house, and rented 8 Morrab Terrace, a tall Regency house with a magnificent view over the beautiful Morrab gardens with its subtropical plants, to the sea and St. Michael's Mount.

It was about this time that sorrow and romance went hand in hand. Grandpa Tyack was paralysed, incontinent and bedridden, due to advanced motor neurone disease, and Mabel got leave from the Royal Bristol Infirmary to come home and nurse him. John Eva, a childhood friend of the family, was home for a holiday after many years ranching in Canada. He was tired of his bachelor life and was looking for a wife to take back with him. At the same time Mabel, who had always said, "I would not give up my nursing for any man," had changed her tune to "I would marry the first man who asked me." The children were highly amused to see the middle-aged courting couple. In the end, John had to return to Canada alone, with the promise that Mabel would follow him as soon as she could, but she refused to leave her dying father.

It was not long before Charles Tyack breathed his last and was laid to rest in Camborne churchyard after a funeral service in Wesley Chapel. The procession that followed him to the grave-side spread up the road and around the town clock. His wife was amazed at the number of strangers who came up to her with accounts of how much they owed to his kindness and help. He left little money, but indeed a rich heritage of care and compassion for the unfortunate.

At last Mabel was free to join her John in Canada. She set off amidst a flurry of excitement, tears and fond farewells. It was arranged that she should be married from Claude's brother Gerald and his wife's home in Calgary, where Gerald was practising as a metallurgist, before setting off across the Rocky Mountains to John's beautiful ranch in British Columbia.

It was a hard life. After so many years on his own, John tended to be stern and taciturn. As soon as it became known that Mabel was a nurse, the sick came flooding to her door and on many occasions she nursed them in her own home with little equipment to help her. There was only one doctor to cover a very large area and if he was called away or on leave, he left his patients in Mabel's care. She delivered the babies, and it was a great joy when at the age of forty-eight, she gave birth to a son of her own.

16

VENEZUELA

Claude's time in Venezuela lasted from 1923 to the early part of 1926. He was employed by The British Controlled Oil Fields, later to be taken over by an American company, The Standard. It was a hard life with only a short break home for Christmas 1924. He led a small expedition into the interior, four Englishmen and a crowd of natives, exploring for oil. It was a lonely life, living in tents, cutting back forests, building roads and bridges as they went, with no social life except the occasional trip to Maracaibo or El Mene. The following are excerpts from a letter to Muriel:

Boxing Day, 1923

Love dear,

I have missed writing to you on Christmas Day. I had settled down to write all the morning and had written the children, when a message came to say that there was a car waiting to take me to Altagracia, as they were loading the tanker. You see love it is the first oil we have ever delivered, or sold if you like, so it was a great occasion and although there was no necessity to go, I thought it would look well if I went down and showed an interest in the company. So off I went and got down about midday. The Shell, or as it is called here, The Caribbean Oil Company was buying our oil and who do you think was measuring it? Well it was young Cunnack from Helston and we introduced ourselves and had a long chat. All our chief officials were there of course and I would have been out of it if I had not gone down. I missed a lovely Christmas dinner by doing so. We only had a snack at

Altagracia although of course we had a glass of champagne in honour of the occasion. Booth, the general manager was coming up. I waited for him and we came back together and we did not get back to the field until ten o'clock at night. We were famished, so that those who had been down to Altagracia and ourselves had a Christmas supper in our mess. It was midnight before we finished. So you see love, I had a funny Christmas. I went 108 kilometres or say 71 miles over an awful road and spent the day watching an oil tanker load. But love it was a famous occasion for not only was it our first delivery, it was also the first cargo of light oil that has ever left Venezuela. We are keeping very quiet about our affairs and there is a lot of curiosity and excitement in Maracaibo, also some jealousy.

This was the most difficult time of Claude's life. The pay was good but he missed Muriel and the children badly and grieved that they were growing up so far away without his care and guidance. There was no air travel uniting families as there is today, and the conditions under which he worked were unsuitable for Muriel and the children. He started work at 6.45 am, returning to camp at about 1.30 pm. During the hot afternoons he stayed is his tent making notes, writing reports and making work schedules. At 5 pm he changed and wrote family letters. 6 pm was dinner-time and a time for relaxation and chat with his English staff until 8 pm. Then more letter writing or reports and an early night.

His letters home were full of love and longing, many of which are preserved and expressed most eloquently his passionate physical and spiritual need of her. Muriel was his love, his childhood sweetheart, his woman, and he desired no other. The following are some extracts from his letters to her:

. . .but darling if we were together do not think that all my love would be passionate and all my expression bodily. Sweet as is the love of lips, eyes and naked limbs and sweet as is the bodily union, there is another side of love and far the greater that will live when our bodies have long since been dead and our passions for ever cold. It is love itself. The joy of our bodies is only the human expression of love.

Love is the thing that has made us one for now and eternity.

> Dearest darling, love I cannot write of tonight, I am too restless and dissatisfied. I want you too much to write about it and dwell on my feelings. It is no longer a joyous pain it is an agony.
>
> Love, my own precious, I want you more than I can say. I want your dear companionship more than I want anything. I had no idea I would miss anyone as much as I miss you. You are the essence of my life. Without you I am but half a man.

It was during this period that Claude decided to offer himself as a candidate for Ordination in the Church of England. He and Muriel were deeply religious and this had been their secret hope since his student days. They were very conscious of the needs of the workers on the oil fields and their families, and he would like to have trained as a worker priest, continuing his work as a consultant geologist, while administering to the spiritual needs of the community. In this he was ahead of his time and the idea was not accepted by the Church of England, although it has now formed an auxiliary priesthood on the lines he envisaged.

In spite of this setback, Muriel negotiated on his behalf with Bishop Frere of Truro, a saintly monk, to obtain his admission to the Theological College at Salisbury for a one year period on condition that he did a certain amount of studying beforehand, including Greek and Latin. The Bishop was most kind and helpful but warned them that as a curate he could not expect more than £200 a year and even as a vicar it might not be more than £300. As Claude was earning £1200 (a very good salary for those days) this would be a great financial sacrifice, especially as he was a married man with four children to educate. After much thought and prayers they decided they could just manage with careful husbandry, without detriment to the children's education. St. Clare's offered reduced fees to the daughters of clergy and Lewis obtained a bursary to St. John's, Leatherhead, a school founded for the sons of the clergy.

Muriel obtained the books advised by the Bishop, posted them to Venezuela, and Claude began to study in earnest, late into the night, by flickering light, in his tent in the forest.

Before Claude returned to England he became very ill and had to be carried by stretcher over rough ground through the forest over 100 miles to the nearest hospital. When he eventually arrived in England he was admitted to the Hospital for Tropical Diseases in London, where it was found he was suffering from severe anaemia due to hookworm. Hookworm is a parasite that inhabits the undergrowth and marshy lands of tropical and subtropical countries. The larvae enter the skin around the ankles and pass through the lymphatics to the blood stream, through the heart to the lungs and up the airways, to be swallowed into the oesophagus and through the stomach to the small intestines, where they attach themselves by hook-like teeth to the mucous membrane, causing haemorrhage, anaemia, debility, dyspepsia and joint pains. The worms are killed by giving anthelmintics which should be harmless to human beings. Claude however was allergic to the drug given and for one hot sunny afternoon lay between life and death. The family in Cornwall were unaware of the danger he had been in until he returned to them.

The following are some of his preliminary notes on the rock drawings of Hombre Pintado which he discovered in the state of Falcon Venezuela:

Preliminary note on the rock drawings of Hombre Pintado in the State of Falcon Venezuela

The rock drawings of Hombre Pintado are of considerable interest, and would repay close study. At a later period I hope to take photographs of the figures, but in case I have not the opportunity the following note is written. They are found on a sandstone face in a gorge about 20 kilometres to the south of Casigua. If it is assumed that the figures were drawn when the bed of the stream was high enough to enable it to be done from the ground we have a rough means of judging their age.

The drawings may be divided into four groups:

1) Primitive drawings about 15 feet above the present bed of the stream.

2) More complex drawings about 10 feet up.

3) Carved representations of footsteps a little lower than the last group.

4) Modern scribblings and initials lower down that are only interesting as an instance of stupidity and vanity. Varieties of the more primitive and higher drawings are shown below:

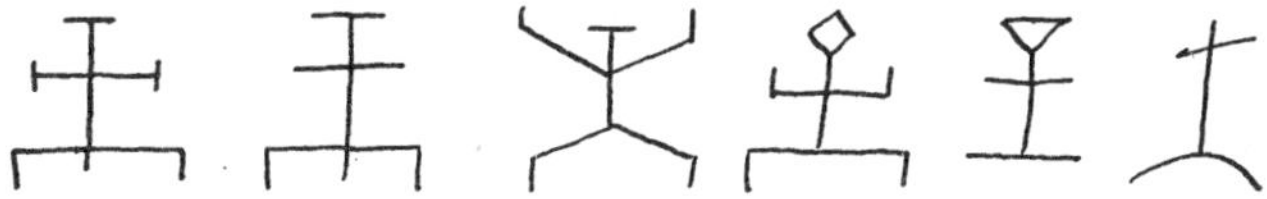

They are exactly similar to the representations of human beings drawn by the late palaeolithic men in Europe, and here it is possible that they are equally ancient for on the supposition adopted the stream must have eroded its bed ten feet since they were drawn and in solid sandstone.

The last figure of a cross on a mound is interesting. There are four or five representations of it in a group just above the figure next to be described. It may be the representation of a female figure as is the figure below, but they remind me of a symbol which I believe occurs in Central America, and which is supposed to refer to the country of origin of the Indians. Its likeness to a symbolic representation of Calvary is obvious, but I think accidental.

Two slightly more complex figures also occur. The first is so obviously a female figure that no comment is necessary. It is also possible that the second is the same as the first symbolised.

The attitudes of these figures is so similar to those of Palaeolithic man, the predynastic Egyptians, and the statuettes of early Crete, Cyprus and Greece that the meaning is probably the same. That is to say they are figures in an attitude of prayer or adoration.

The second group consists of five drawings situated just below the first group. Two of these drawings represent human beings - one a male and the other a female. The other three are somewhat similar to the Greek key ornament. Four of the forms are roughly drawn below:

The first figure is very much better drawn than the second and it is higher up on the rock. It is so much better drawn that one is at once suspicious that the second is a forgery; but certain differences in the figures do not support this conclusion . . .

This is all of the notes that have survived and unfortunately they are incomplete.

17

LOOE

In the autumn of 1926 Claude Sara entered the Theological College at Salisbury as a mature student, for a year's intensive course. It must have been a great change from the oil fields. The family remained at Morrab Terrace in Penzance. It was a time during which strict economy had to be practised, but it was wonderful to be together during the holidays.

It was during this time that Ivy left to be married to a railway worker from Swindon. Each year a crowd of young men would come down from Swindon for their holidays. Muriel approved of the young man and allowed Ivy to entertain him in the breakfast room, rather than roaming the streets late at night. The children were enthralled with the romance.

Miss Mitchell, a distant connection of the Tyack family came to stay as a paying guest, while she was commissioned to draw up the family tree of the Lanyon family (original spelling Lan-i-on) which went back to 1244 when they came over from France as courtiers and were given lands in Madron and Gwinear in the county of Cornwall. Muriel's great-grandmother Mary Lanyon (1782-1823) had been a member of the Gwinear branch. Miss Mitchell presented Muriel with a copy of this branch, which is now in the possession of her daughter Betty (Elizabeth Flawn). Miss Mitchell hoped that the family tree would be passed by the House of Heralds but she died tragically before this could be accomplished. She was run over by a train and killed instantly, while picking flowers on a railway cutting at St. Columb.

Miss Mitchell was small, dumpy and insignificant looking, but possessed of great intelligence and was an interesting story teller. Betty loved to talk to her but the other children were not interested. They would spend hours by the fire in her bed-sitting room, Betty completely enthralled by the tales she had to tell, especially of when her fairy godmother appeared to her.

The Sara grandparents had now moved to 4 Tretorvac Terrace, Heamoor. Grandpa frequently walked down from Heamoor to visit his grandchildren at 8 Morrab Terrace. He enjoyed taking them to tea at Chirgwin's restaurant at the top of Market Jew Street and feeding them with fluffy cream buns.

As Chy-an-Towan, which was in reality Claude's property, was now empty, Muriel and the children used it as a holiday home and spent many happy holidays there. However, Butcher Reynolds and his wife lived next door and Mrs Reynolds wanted it as a home for her sister, and pestered Muriel so much that eventually she gave way and sold it to them. Half an hour after signing the deeds of transfer, a cable arrived from Claude, 'Don't sell'. The children too were very upset at losing their lovely holiday home. So Muriel bought them a houseboat on Hayle estuary.

The houseboat was a converted fishing lugger, with bunks in the hold and a small galley at one end. Cooking and lighting were done by paraffin which was very smelly. On a sand bank opposite was a little wooden hut containing a chemical closet. The children found it great fun. They would set off at the beginning of spring and summer holidays from Penzance station to Hayle, like gypsies, in their oldest clothes, with pots and pans slung about their person. Aunty Katy and Granny Tyack bought the next boathouse and as Granny was in a wheelchair, it was a tremendous undertaking getting her in and out. When Claude returned from Venezuela, the houseboat was replaced by a chalet which however was not nearly as much fun.

Towards the end of Claude's year at Theological College, Mr Hyde-Less, the vicar of Looe in south east Cornwall, offered him the post of curate. So a busy time followed, packing up house at Penzance, and finding somewhere to live in Looe. Muriel's health was very poor. Ivy had left and Claude was still at Salisbury taking exams. Ia was busy with school affairs, so it was left to Betty to help her mother. Muriel was not methodical or domesticated so it was all a bit chaotic, with things stuffed into trunks willy-nilly and the children sitting on top to close them.

Claude was ordained at Truro cathedral on Trinity Sunday 1927. He spent a few days beforehand in retreat at Les Escop, the bishop's palace.

A large car was ordered to take the family to Truro, first picking up Claude's parents at Heamoor as the service was at 7 am, and they had to be there in good time beforehand. The car was ordered for 5.30 am. Muriel wanted all the children to look smart and a credit to their father and it was no easy matter to have four children up and dressed by 5.30 am. All the clothes were set out the night before. Ia had a new hat which was very becoming. Lewis' suit had been sponged and pressed, he was to make his first communion and she hoped he would keep his socks pulled up. At last they were ready and the car was on time. As they got in Granny Sara who was very particular, eyed them critically, then nodded in approval. Muriel sighed in relief, they had passed the acid test and all her hard work had not been in vain. They stopped at Camborne to pick up Aunty Katy, and arrived at the cathedral in good time.

It was a magnificent service and the children were most impressed. Afterwards they were invited to a wonderful breakfast at Les Escop, where the bishop waited on them and was most kind and fatherly.

Lady Ebury invited Ia and Betty to stay with her for the last six weeks of the summer term in her house in Marazion. She drove them to school and back each day. It was arranged that they would be boarders in the autumn.

Lewis and Nadia accompanied their parents to Looe. Lewis was to be a pupil at St. John's Leatherhead, a school for clergy sons, in September. Granny Tyack implored them not to send him to boarding school, saying he would die if they did, a prediction which tragically became true. Claude, who had always felt some inferiority because he had only been to grammar school himself was determined that his children should have the benefit of a public school education, feeling that a good education was the finest gift a father could give his children. Whatever else was sacrificed their education must not suffer.

Claude and Muriel rented a three storey house up a steep hill overlooking the harbour and river, 4 Whitlieburn Terrace. Across the road there was a building with a flat roof on which the sea-gulls gathered. One always sat on the chimneypot like a schoolteacher while the others arranged themselves like pupils in straight lines below. Looe is a beautiful fishing village lying in a valley. It is separated into East and West Looe by a river, which meandered through glorious countryside to a little wood where the children loved to wander and find rare wild flowers. It may be built over by now.

Lewis made friends with the seafaring community and loved to listen to their tales. He was given the use of an old rowing boat and they had many excursions up the river. It was a leaky boat and Betty spent most of her time bailing out. When the sun shone during the holidays, as soon as their chores were finished, Claude would send the children on to the beach. Hannifore beach was secluded and safe. It had fascinating rocky pools which the children loved to explore. At lunch time, if well enough, Muriel would arrive with a basket of hot pasties. On Thursday afternoons, much to the children's amusement, the beach would be invaded by a horde of local mums and their children, armed with towels and soap for the children's weekly bath. Clothes were stripped off and there was a great business of back scrubbing amidst shrieks from the children at the coldness of the water. They were happy sunny days soon to be followed by tragedy.

Old Captain Walters loved to take Lewis fishing, so he would get up at 5 am to do his chores, take mother a cup of tea and be off, bringing back some lovely fish for tea. When Lewis died, the old captain was so heartbroken he gave up fishing and sold his boat.

The village people, knowing that the Sara's had four children to feed, would leave fish and garden produce, particularly runner beans, on their doorstep. They never knew when they opened the door, what they would find. Muriel got the children sitting around the dining-room table cutting up beans by the hour, a job they hated. They were then salted down in large earthenware jars for the winter. Unfortunately when they came out they were very salty, discoloured and rather unpleasant, nevertheless, no one was excused from eating them. Eggs, only sixpence a dozen in the spring, were stored in isinglass and had a peculiar taste.

Lewis was a handsome boy, tall and well built. He had thick, wavy dark hair, perfect skin, laughing black eyes and a generous mouth. He was the joy of his mother's heart and he adored her. He could not bear to see her doing heavy, unfamiliar work. They were without domestic help, and during school holidays he did all he could to relieve her. On wash days, even if he was out with his friends, he would excuse himself and rush home to turn the mangle. He loved cooking and in a white apron, would preside over the frying pan. Making sweets was another specialty and on one occasion he made a lot of sloe wine which proved very potent. Muriel bought a steam cooker with great difficulty, as it was something new and almost unobtainable, but she eventually tracked one down at Spooners in Plymouth. Lewis loved to use it. Claude was annoyed by Lewis' fondness for cooking, thinking it an unmanly occupation. He always tended to be severe with the boy, as he feared being brought up in a family of girls, he might be spoiled and soft.

He need not have feared. Lewis enjoyed athletics, he was the fastest runner in the school, good at swimming and boxing. He had a good sense of humour and was full of fun. Although not particularly academic, he excelled at mathematics and general knowledge. Betty and he had a very close relationship and were often mistaken for twins. Although despising schoolgirls in general he would say to her. "You're different, you understand boys." She got on well with his companions but was shy of the girls her own age. He was her champion. One day when they were walking down the back lane, a boy made a face at her and before the boy could draw breath, Lewis had knocked him flat on the ground.

Life at Looe was very hard for Muriel and Claude Sara. In fact, in spite of the beauty surrounding them, it was the most tragic time of their lives. Money was very scarce. The three storied house was inconvenient and she was bleeding heavily from a fibroid tumour. Operations were less common in those days and greatly feared. She spent at least a fortnight in every month in bed with the foot of the bed raised. Pads were insufficient and old sheets were used in an attempt to absorb the blood. Betty begged to be allowed to leave school to look after her mother, but this her father would not allow. He took on the nursing himself and was sometimes in despair that after all his long years in the wilderness he would lose his beloved wife.

Ia had left school due to ill health and had been sent to stay with her Uncle Teddy Sara in London in order to obtain specialist advice, after which it was decided to send her for a prolonged visit to friends in Scotland, in order to recuperate. Teddy was at that time, vicar of St. John's, Walham Green in Fulham, and lived with his wife Mary in a beautiful Queen Anne house. Much to their mutual regret they had no children.

In July 1929, news arrived from St. John's School Leatherhead, that Lewis was suffering from blood poisoning due to pricking his finger with a compass, and had been admitted to St. Luke's nursing home for clergy families in London. It was the beginning of the summer holidays and when Betty arrived at Looe station, she found her mother walking on the platform with her suitcase packed, ready to leave on the train that she had just vacated, for London via Lostwithiel. It was a tragic homecoming. With a hasty kiss and instructions to look after Claude and Nadia, Muriel was off.

Anxious days followed. Muriel stayed with her brother in-law Teddy Sara. His wife was on her annual visit to Dublin, visiting her parents. The maid was on holiday. Teddy and his live-in curate Mr Hopkins, looked after her as well as they could. She was very ill, losing blood heavily and having to wear a mackintosh in spite of a heatwave on her daily bus rides to St. Luke's nursing home, arriving back to Walham Green in a state of near collapse.

The doctors were making a heroic fight for Lewis' life, there were at that time no antibiotics or sulphur drugs that could help him. One finger was amputated and then half his hand, there was talk of removing his arm. Lewis put up a brave fight and showed loving concern for his mother; but in spite of all efforts his condition worsened. It was a heartbreaking time for Muriel, watching her beloved son becoming weaker and weaker. He was like a skeleton, but she never gave up hope.

In Looe, Betty was trying her best to run the house and look after Claude and Nadia. Claude gave her a pound for weekly housekeeping on which she managed, but became very upset when she found she was half a penny short in her accounts.

August Bank holiday (then at the beginning of the month) was a glorious sunny day, with Looe looking at its most beautiful. Because of the tide, the regatta was held in the evening and was in full swing, when a telegram arrived for Claude, 'Come at once.' He was in bed with a recurrence of fever, sleeping with blinds drawn. Betty roused her father, helped him to pack and catch the late night train for London.

Claude was worried at leaving his two young daughters alone in the house overnight, and made Betty promise to send for Aunty Katy in the morning. She arrived about midday and was a great comfort to the girls. Everyone was very kind, especially Mrs Bidwell, wife of a retired Colonel in the Indian Army, whose son was a great friend of Lewis. Will Allsup, a retired owner of a shipyard in Preston, who had shown great interest in Lewis, called each day and arranged little outings for the girls, bringing with him a bunch of rosebuds from his garden.

Betty went to the 8 am Holy Communion at St. Nicholas church daily to pray for her brother. Then came the morning when it became impossible to pray for her brother's recovery, as hard as she tried, she could not. She ran home in self disgust as soon as the service was over, not waiting to speak to the Vicar, as was her custom. The Vicar followed soon after to tell her that he had had a telephone call that Lewis was dead. He was very kind and she was never to forget his advice to keep herself busy.

"Polish your sorrow into the wood," he said. So she worked hard polishing all the furniture, filling the house with flowers and refusing to draw the blinds, which was the custom, and rather shocked Aunty Katy. If Lewis could look down on his home she wanted him to see it at its best.

Nadia, who was only eleven, slept late and Betty would not wake her. Mrs Gregg, who lived on a farm in a beautiful manor house and had a daughter Rosemary about Nadia's age, invited her to stay. It was a brilliantly sunny day and as Nadia and Betty who accompanied her, walked up to the farm, the glory of the sun and the beauty of the countryside seemed to mock them.

A requiem at St. John's church Walham Green was followed by burial at East Sheen cemetery. The only members of the family present were Claude, Muriel and Teddy Sara.

Soon after returning to Cornwall, it was decided to examine Muriel under anaesthetic, with the possibility of performing a hysterectomy, however major surgery was decided against. While under anaesthetic she seemed to be in a wonderful place full of light, beautiful flowers and sweet music. Lewis was there and so happy that she begged to stay with him. Lewis said, "You must go back, you have work to do." As soon as she came round from the anaesthetic, the theatre sister heard her murmuring, "Lewis let me stay with you."

It was decided that Nadia, who had been attending a small private school in Looe, should become a boarder at St. Dunstan's Abbey in Plymouth, run by an order of Anglican nuns. The nuns were very kind to the girls and it was a school with a good reputation. Nadia got on well with the other pupils and was happy there.

Ia returned from Scotland and started working at the nursing home. The matron Mrs Tucker, was a friend of the family and her granddaughter Miriam, who spent her holidays with her grandmother, was a constant companion of the Sara children.

Ia's time at the nursing home was not to be long. Will Allsup became interested in her. He lived in a modern bungalow, surrounded by a beautiful garden, close to the nursing home. By Christmas they were engaged. Ia was only nineteen and Will over fifty, older than her father. Muriel was very much against the engagement, but her objections were overruled. Claude, remembering the objections there had been to his own marriage, gave consent. As Will was a wealthy man, the Sara grandparents thought it a good match, and even Uncle Teddy was in favour.

Ia Sara was married to William Allsup the following year, June 1930. She wore white and carried red roses. It was a quiet wedding at St. Nicholas church, followed by a reception at home. Betty and Nadia were given time off from school to attend. It proved to be a tragic affair. Will was very kind to her, treating her more like a daughter than a wife. She had a recurrence of her old illness and a complete breakdown in health from which she never recovered.

The Saras spent one more year in Looe and then Claude was offered the living of St. Dennis, near St. Austell.

The grandparents Adah and William Sara had for some years been living in the lovely old vicarage at St. Veep. Their faithful maid Gladys moved with them. She was married from their home, and was given a lovely reception. Her husband moved in as gardener and chauffeur. Betty and Nadia spent many enjoyable holidays with their grandparents. Betty was very fond of Gladys and their daily help, and Granny would get rather cross saying, "Betty prefers kitchen company," and in fact she did, as she was a little scared of Granny. They were on one occasion taken to a rather smart tea party. There was lovely food provided which was pressed upon them, being the only children present. They were feeling very hungry but for politeness sake, accepted one small sandwich and an iced cake, and felt very upset when on their return, Granny reprimanded them for overeating.

18

ST. DENNIS

In the nineteen-thirties St. Dennis was a stark, moorland village set in the middle of the clay mining district of St. Austell. It was surrounded by white mountains of sand waste, which on moonlight nights gave off a strange beauty. The rectory and garden were in a valley, like an oasis in the middle of all this harshness. It was a mellow square house covered with virginia creeper. The garden was a joy to all the village and open to all on Sunday evenings after church. There were large lawns, including a tennis court, flower beds, flowering shrubs and two orchards. In the spring hundreds of daffodils grew among the apple trees in the lower orchard. A secluded little rose garden was the ideal place for afternoon tea or retreat with a book, it seemed a haven of tranquillity. Tall trees grew on either side of the drive. There was a large vegetable garden, including numerous crops of raspberries. Hidden in the bushes was a piggery. The sexton Mr Stribly, looked after the garden, when he was not digging graves, it was his pride and joy.

It was a steep climb up to the church, through several fields, or a longer way around through the village. The church stood in splendid isolation at the top of a high hill and was a landmark for miles around. It is said to be built on the site of an old Arthurian castle, Demelioc, the place of Arthur's conception. It is surrounded by a circular churchyard and what looks like the remains of a moat. The church had a Norman font and an ancient British granite cross stood in the churchyard. The old church was destroyed by arson in the nineteen-eighties. It is now rebuilt.

The Sara family arrived in St. Dennis in July 1931. Betty had completed her time at school and came by bus from Penzance. It seemed as if she was going into a desolate country, a far cry from the beauty of Looe. Pamela, a companion from school who was from a one parent family, was spending the school holidays with the Sara family, by an arrangement with the headmistress of St. Clare's.

It was said of the people of St. Dennis, that if they liked you they could not do enough for you, but if they disliked you, you might as well be dead. Fortunately they took the Saras to their hearts.

St. Dennis was in the middle of the depression of the thirties. The village was made up chiefly of clay workers, many of whom were out of work. Poverty was rife. Muriel collected a room full of second hand clothes, begged from her friends, which she gave freely to those in need. The rectory door was open at all times to any of the villagers, whatever their faith or lack of it. Claude considered them all part of his family and he and Muriel made a habit of visiting every afternoon. Where there was severe illness they would visit daily and would sometimes sit up all night with the dying. Claude would even be prepared to return from his holidays to visit a sick person.

Tuberculosis was rife in the village. It was tragic to see the young people die. The girls were so pretty and the boys handsome. It was said that the fluff from the wool factory where the girls worked, was a contributory factor. It was a musical village and Madge, the Taylors' daughter, known as the Cornish nightingale because of her beautiful voice, caught the disease from her brother and they both died of it. There was no specific treatment for tuberculosis in those days. Then Norah, the youngest, who was also making a name for herself as a singer, was found to be infected, but the disease was caught in time and she was treated at the Brompton Hospital. She survived but had to give up her singing career. All this became too much for their heartbroken father and he died of a stroke. Claude and Muriel upheld them all in their troubles, in spite of their being Chapel. The Saras would not leave the parish for a day before visiting the grief stricken family.

It was the days before the national health service, but St. Dennis was blessed with a much loved doctor and his wife. Dr and Mrs Manson were the very heart of the village, and in almost any cottage one entered, their photograph took pride of place on the mantelpiece. They were brimming over with love for each other and tender care for their patients. Although Mrs Manson was an invalid and spent many months in bed, she was full of fun, was up to date with all the news and took an active interest in all village affairs.

As the welfare state was not in existence then, the villagers turned to doctor or parson in time of need. If an unmarried girl became pregnant, Dr Manson was hot on the heels of the father of the child and made him do his duty as a man.

Dr Manson was on call night and day. Mrs Manson never knew when to expect him and he often left a meal half eaten in response to an urgent call. He did his own dispensing with the aid of a village girl.

Dr Manson and his wife had private means. He rarely sent in bills and never to the rectory. It was considered unethical in those days to charge clergy families medical fees.

Before the days of the bingo halls and television, the village had to provide its own entertainment by means of homemade concerts, dances in the village hall and an occasional whist-drive. Being a musical village, it was and still is, famous for its band. One of the joys of Christmas was to be woken up at dawn to the sound of carols being rung out by hand bells in the rectory garden.

Dagmar Hancock, who taught at the village school, played an important part in organising village activities. She formed a Girl Guide and Ranger company, making Betty her Lieutenant, for the eighteen months she was at home, before starting her nursing career. Dagmar also produced a first class Christmas pantomime for many years, teaching the dancing and making the costumes herself. She also formed a women's hockey team and arranged matches with surrounding villages.

Money was scarce in the Sara household, the rector's stipend being only £400 a year, of which £100 was deducted towards the pension of the retired rector. The system of tithing was still in operation and there was a tithe farm attached to the rectory.

The rectory was large. It required a lot of heating and upkeep. Muriel was assisted in the house by a number of school leavers who were of doubtful help. Her mainstay was Mrs Wilson with her smiling, jovial face. There was something very comfortable about Mrs Wilson, she became part of the family and remained so for the rest of Claude and Muriel's lifetime. Mother of a large family, she would arrive with a baby in the pram.

In the First World War Mr Wilson had been reported missing, presumed dead. Mrs Wilson, young and pretty, had struck up a friendship with another man, they became engaged and on the eve of their wedding, her long lost husband returned to claim her. They settled down quite happily again; but on the piano in her front room, pride of place was given to her ex-fiancée. She would say with a laugh, "That is the man I was going to marry," and her husband did not seem to mind.

One of the highlights of the year was the garden fete held in the rectory garden. It always seemed to be a sunny day and there would be a hectic putting up of stalls and bunting. Sam Eva, chairman of the Pig Marketing Board, and Muriel's cousin and admirer, would donate a pig for auction. There was pandemonium when the pig escaped and was chased all over the garden. Someone of note would have been invited to open the fête. In the middle of all the chaos Muriel would sally forth, serene and unperturbed in her picture hat and flowing floral gown, to greet the important person.

As well as being governor of the church school to which he made frequent visits, Claude was rural district councillor and took an active interest in the welfare of the community. In those days council work was unpaid. He was especially concerned with housing and the plight of the poor and needy. Muriel became 'enrolling member' of the Mother's Union, and was in great demand as a speaker for them and the Women's Institute. She found she had a flair for public speaking and thoroughly enjoyed it. Through this she made many friends in the county and it added greatly to her social life. Muriel had a gregarious nature and loved people from all walks of life. Claude on the other hand, was a modest, retiring man, but was a true and sympathetic friend to those in need and would take endless trouble on their behalf.

Muriel Sara also started 'The Girl's Friendly Society' (G.F.S.), who met weekly at the rectory. For the boys she organised 'Kings Messengers'. They were rather naughty boys and Muriel was no disciplinarian, but she liked little boys, having lost her only son, and a happy riotous time was had by all. If the house became rather untidy, it did not really matter. A home was for living in not a museum, was her motto.

In the summer there was a large raspberry crop and in the height of the season, Claude would pick as many as seventy pounds of raspberries a day which Muriel would sell to the hotels in Newquay. It was exhausting work but it paid for the upkeep of the garden and Stribly's wage.

In spite of their many hardships and lack of money, Claude and Muriel never complained and entered heart and soul into the life of the parish.

In August 1932 Betty spent a month in London with her uncle, the vicar of Walham Green in Fulham. To her it was all a great adventure and she was fascinated with London. The Rev. Edmund Sara (Uncle Teddy) was a very busy man, with a large parish to look after and a lot of committee meetings. Aunt Mary was on her annual visit to Dublin and Betty was left to a large extent in the housekeeper Amy's care. They enjoyed each other's company and became life long friends. Amy showed her the sights of London. There was no nonsense about Amy and she was never afraid to speak her mind. She was a loyal member of the household with a particular affection for its mistress, and accompanied them to Jamaica when Edmund Sara became assistant bishop of that island.

In spite of his busy schedule, Uncle Teddy arranged with his large circle of friends, outings and treats for his young niece. One morning at breakfast he said to her, "What are you going to do with your life? You are not going to stay home and grow old like a cabbage are you?"

To which she replied, "I thought I might like to be a nurse."

Teddy Sara was not one to let grass grow under his feet. He said, "You must go to Bart's." And by lunch time she had been shown over the hospital by Marjory Goodsell, matron's secretary, who had been his secretary at the Sunday School Institute before training as a nurse. Betty was most impressed and left with a brochure of the hospital and an application form, which she did not fill in until she returned home and was able to discuss it with her parents.

In November she had an interview at St. Bartholomew's Hospital. By this time Teddy Sara was appointed chancellor of Truro cathedral, and had moved from Walham Green to Benson

House in Truro, but he arranged for Betty to stay with some of his many friends.

An unexpected vacancy occurred in January 1933 and so there was a hectic rush to get uniforms which had to be specially ordered from Arnold's of London; four grey dresses, sixteen aprons, twelve stiff collars (which cut into the neck) and twelve pairs of cuffs and twelve caps, all of which had to be paid for by the applicant and her family, as well as the fee for six weeks preliminary training school. After this trial period, if she was accepted she received twenty pounds for the first year, paid quarterly.

It was a dank January day when Betty was driven in late afternoon from Paddington station, in a musty smelling horse-drawn hansom cab to King's Square, Goswell Road, near the Angel Islington. The Preliminary Training School was situated in a quiet square of elegant houses in the midst of the slums of north London.

The school was made up of twenty young ladies from sheltered backgrounds. Miss Field, the Sister in charge, was a very gracious lady, small, slim, young and very attractive in her spotless uniform. Underneath the charming exterior there was strength of character and a strong will. She was kind but firm, with very high ideals, which she imparted to her young hopefuls. She would stand no slackness and was a person to be reckoned with.

On the first evening the girls were shown how to make up and put on their caps, no hair was allowed to show. They were presented with hospital cloaks of black serge lined with red. If they completed their four years training, the cloaks were theirs to keep and become a symbol of pride. If not, they had to be returned. One of their first tasks was to embroider their name in black wool on the inside of the collar, to be inspected by Miss Field. They also had to sew laundry numbers on to their uniforms. The dresses had to be exactly six inches from the floor and the aprons two inches shorter, all of which was measured exactly by Miss Field. Black woollen stockings were worn and black laced shoes with two inch rubber soled heels.

Betty never forgot Miss Fields' first lecture on 'Ethics of Nursing', when she said, "No one forces you to be a nurse, but if you do become a nurse you take on the responsibility of life and death and can never lay it down. If you are not prepared to accept this responsibility leave now." It was an awesome challenge.

The girls were a friendly group and Betty lost her shyness with them. She enjoyed the school very much. It was a very intensive course. At weekends the girls explored London mostly on foot, as they were all short of money. It was all new and exciting.

At the end of six weeks they were examined, both in theory and practice, and only if they passed and were considered suitable by Miss Fellows, were they admitted to the hospital for training for a three month trial period.

After this trial period they were up for 'Elections'.This was an awesome occasion, when the poor terrified girl had to appear before the Board of Governors. The beadle ushered her in through the outer door of the boardroom as Miss so and so. The chairman either said, "We have great pleasure in electing you to the staff of the hospital", or "We regret we cannot elect you to the staff of the hospital." On rare occasions an extra three months trial was allowed. If the candidate was elected, she was ushered out through the inner door as nurse. If not, she had to go through the door through which she had entered.

Betty had her tonsils removed on 'Election Day' and was elected without being present, which was quite unheard of, but she felt that tonsillectomy was to be preferred to the frightening 'Elections'.

No one knew until they entered the boardroom what their fate would be; but even after elections, one was not safe from instant dismissal, if one's work or behaviour was not up to standard. Home Sister was a tyrant who seemed to have eyes in the back of her head. She carried a tape measure to make sure that uniform dresses were exactly six inches from the ground and aprons two inches shorter. Woe betide the nurse who showed hair under her cap, or had a hole in the heel of her black woollen stocking. The home was an attractive place with nice individual rooms, but only five articles were allowed on the dressing table.

Miss Day, the matron, was young and modern for the day. She was attractive and queen-like in appearance. She did not make a lot of petty rules, but expected a high standard of behaviour; emphasising that Barts was the oldest hospital in the British Empire, with eight hundred years of tradition, and it was a great privilege to train there. Friendship between nurses and medical students was allowed as long as it was in the open and they behaved themselves. Above all, she valued kindness to the patients, and a nurse who was abrupt or rough in her manner, was never given a second chance. She would say, "I can teach a nurse to be efficient, I can teach her to be quick, but I cannot teach her to be kind. That is a quality that she must bring with her."

Barts was a very friendly, happy hospital. The nurses had a saying: "If you want to be a lady go to Thomas'. If you want to get married go to Guy's, if you want to be a nurse, come to Barts."

In 1935, Muriel and Claude were invited to an Oxford Group house party (later known as Moral Re-armament, M.R.A.) to be held at one of the Oxford colleges. At first he declined the invitation, pleading over work, as he considered the whole thing "a lot of damned nonsense". However he was invited again at a later date, and feeling he could not offer the same excuse, accepted with great reluctance.

This became a turning point in his life and that of Muriel and the family. Following the sacrifice of his successful career, there had been so many sorrows and hardships, that he had become very depressed. Due to his contact with the Oxford Group, Claude received a new vision and outpouring of spiritual strength. Their happiness and radiant faces impressed him, and their insistence that God had a plan for every man and every nation, if only they would listen to the guidance of the Holy Spirit speaking within their heart.

The way to receive guidance was first to surrender one's life to God and then to seek His will daily in a morning quiet time, and writing down the thoughts that came. Team work, checking and sharing one's thoughts was an important part. Also endeavouring to live one's life by the four standards of absolute honesty, absolute purity, absolute unselfishness and absolute love. It was also necessary to make restitution as far as possible to anyone whom one had wronged.

Following the house party at Oxford, Claude was invited to accompany the team to Denmark, which he found most inspiring. On returning to England, he broke his Journey in London to visit Betty and she was most impressed to see her beloved father looking ten years younger and with a new glow on his face.

St. Dennis rectory became a place of joy and hospitality as it had never been before. Claude became one of the leaders of the Oxford Group movement in Cornwall, and the rectory was a centre for meetings and house parties.

At Easter 1936, Betty came home on leave from St. Bartholomew's hospital and was, with great reluctance, taken by her parents to a weekend Oxford Group house party in Plymouth. This changed her life. Her health, which had been so poor that it had been doubtful if she would be able to complete her training, improved. On her return to hospital, her friends kept saying "How well you look". Her life became more positive. She was able to complete her general and midwifery training, face up to the rigours of wartime London and become a registered nurse tutor.

19

THE SECOND WORLD WAR

September 1939 saw the outbreak of the Second World War. There was a wave of patriotism throughout the country, a tremendous feeling of comradeship, and determination to do all in one's power to support the war effort.

The tennis court at the St. Dennis rectory was dug up and planted with potatoes, in response to the slogan 'Dig for victory'. A pig was installed in the disused pigsty, there were beehives in the lower orchard and the upper orchard was fenced in to make a chicken run to help with food shortages.

Claude Sara became very busy with committee meetings, arranging for receptions, housing and care of evacuees from London. Muriel joined the local Red Cross and was very proud of her uniform.

Betty Sara, having completed both her general and midwifery training, was working in the East End of London, at St. Mary's hospital, Plaistow, which was on the direct route to the Albert docks, a prime target for enemy bombardment. St. Mary's had been a very pretty Women's and Children's hospital, but became a casualty clearing station, and during the height of the blitz, was the only hospital able to take stretcher cases in the large boroughs of East and West Ham. For some days before the outbreak of war, the staff, from doctors to domestics had been heroically filling sand bags to fortify the hospital.

The memory of the children marching out of London, school by school, to an unknown destination, with their labels, carrying their gas masks and a suitcase, still brings tears to Betty's eyes.

During the early part of the blitz, the only safe place was the hospital basement. Beds were placed along the passages. Clean surgical cases and air-raid casualties, blood stained and dirty, all had to be nursed together, some on beds and some on mattresses under the beds. People from surrounding houses and small shops also sheltered there for safety. To quote one of them, "We feel the angels' wings over the hospital." Later the windows of the ground floor wards were bricked up and patients could be nursed in them, although they were transferred to safer hospitals in the country as soon as possible. The upper floors were abandoned.

Nadia had taken a post as chauffeuse and companion to a family in Pinner. When the war broke out, she and Barbara, the daughter of the house, joined the ambulance service, but they were never called out. Later in the war she went to Sheffield as companion and chauffeuse to some elderly friends and did war work in a factory owned by them, for making cutting tools.

Gerald Sara had opened an office in Calgary as a consultant metallurgist. One day, some trappers from Great Bear Lake brought him a substance for analysis, which he found to contain pitch-blende, a black oxide of uranium. He immediately informed the Canadian Government of his find and was sent to England by them, with letters for the British Government. It was during the early part of the war and very hush hush.

While he was with his parents in Cornwall, he developed a severe and persistent sore throat which proved to be cancer of the larynx. After receiving a course of radiotherapy at St. Bartholomew's hospital, he worked in a high security laboratory in the Midlands, where later it was found that they were doing research on splitting the atom, which led to the formation of the atom bomb. The cancer recurred, and he and his wife May were given a home at St. Dennis rectory. He had a very dreadful and prolonged death through which he was nursed with great love and devotion by his wife. His dying words to her were, "I hope the experiments on which I have been working will never be completed as they will change the face of the earth."

It was a very hard time for Claude and Muriel Sara. Food and fuel were rationed and it was difficult to keep the rectory with its large and lofty rooms, warm. Not only had they given refuge to

Gerald and his wife, but Claude's parents were getting very old and his mother confused, so they too were given a home during their last days.

Muriel's health was poor and help was scarce. The only bright light on the horizon was the arrival of Emily Neat, a middle-aged spinster and retired seamstress, evacuated from London. She immediately became one of the family and was the mainstay for a number of years. Emily had a cockney sense of humour. She was good with the old people, helped with cooking, housework and mending. The hens were her particular joy and she loved to feed them and go out into the orchard to talk to them. Being a Londoner, she found the countryside fascinating.

As well as Claude's parents, Muriel's mother, Elizabeth Tyack, was getting very feeble. She died peacefully in her home at Camborne a month before her ninetieth birthday. Her mind was as clear as a bell and she went to sleep gently, with a prayer upon her lips. A few weeks previously, when Betty, on leave from hospital, had visited her, she said, "You won't see me again dear. My time has come."

It was a glorious sunny Saturday. Betty and Nadia met for a day's outing in the West End. Betty was by now Night Sister at St. Mary's and had a weekend off. Nadia was living with the Betts at Pinner. After window shopping and a light snack, they decided to go to the midday showing of *Gone With the Wind* at the Leicester Square Odeon. They were enthralled with the film, but when they came out, London was almost 'gone with the wind'. The blitz had started in earnest. The sky over the East End was red with fire.

They arranged to visit Uncle Gerald and Aunt May at Gloucester Road where they were lodging, while Uncle Gerald was receiving radiotherapy at Barts. After tea the blitz got worse and Uncle begged the girls to spend the night with them. After ringing up Matron, Betty said, "I must try to get back, but if it is impossible, I will return."

Aunt May's nephew, an air-raid warden, saw them off at Gloucester Road station. Nadia, going north to Pinner only just missed a bomb, and Betty going east to Plaistow. They wondered if they would ever meet again. The trains going east stopped at Aldgate East, but Betty got a lift in an A.R.P. car. One road was blocked by a fire, another by an unexploded bomb. It was like driving into a fiery furnace.

At the hospital there were dead and dying everywhere. It was not possible to give an accurate statement of the number - mangled bodies, and children with their brains hanging out. In the morning, there were pathetic groups of people wandering from hospital to hospital trying to find their dear ones.

After this nightmare night, Holy Communion was celebrated in one of the wards, the staff in their dirty and bloodstained uniforms.

The following is an extract of a letter written by Betty to her parents the following Monday.

St. Mary's Hospital for
Women and Children,
Upper Road,
Plaistow E 13.

Early Monday evening

My Dearests,

Don't be anxious about me. So far things have not hurt us. We have been wonderfully protected.

It is no good pretending that nothing has happened. It was very pathetic seeing the homeless walking around the streets yesterday morning, also the casualties and the people brought in dead. The fires were most terrifying of all.

I was over at Uncle Gerald's when the fires broke out and had to come back during a raid between about nine and ten pm. After a certain point there were no trains running. It seemed madness to try and get back, but I had been asked by Matron to try, and the old discipline of obeying orders held, so I tried.

Luckily someone stopped an A.R.P. car which was coming my way and I came back in that. It was an experience which one will never forget. The glow from the fires was as light almost as day.

One of the A.R.P. men said to me, "You're a very cool sort of female," and I said, "I happen to believe in God, and besides it is not any good being anything else." But it did seem very eerie and as if we were driving to the end of the world.

We had a very busy night. It was really my weekend off.

I do not really feel that I shall get hurt in these raids. I feel

God's plan for me isn't fulfilled yet, but in any case we can only die once and it is better to die doing one's duty, than being a coward. The words of this hymn were with me last night.

'Death will come one day to me,
Saviour keep me close to thee.
Dying may I still abide
In thy heart and wounded side.'

It is wonderful the strength and confidence which comes from God and how in a crisis we feel His peace.

We are all in the basement. I am sitting down for a few minutes to have a rest in case when the 'All Clear' sounds, we are busy with casualties. We have all our patients down here, children, women, also male casualties, and neighbours come in for refuge.

If anything should happen to me, and I don't feel it will, don't be unhappy.

One night, sixteen landmines were dropped around the hospital. Another night, there was a severe fire bomb raid. Orders were given to transfer the operating theatre to a basement across the road. All available staff including domestics, could be seen rushing across the road with pieces of equipment, in spite of bombs, and having no tin hats; and within half an hour, operations were taking place in the makeshift theatre. For that night's work the hospital was given a letter of commendation. In the meanwhile the nurses were frantically trying to extinguish fires surrounding the hospital. The nearby cottages were in ruins and evacuated, but the fires illuminated the hospital and were a guide to enemy planes. By the time the firemen arrived, all the fires were out except one on the roof which the nurses could not reach.

The dead as well as the injured were brought into the hospital and the corpses laid as they were, on the concrete floor of the incomplete new outpatients' building. Although it was partially covered, it was open to the winds, and early in the morning, Betty and a nurse had, by the light of a hurricane lantern, to write a description of the corpses. As well as being a gruesome task with the wind howling around, it was difficult to give an accurate description, as they were all covered with grey dust. At 8 am a mounted policeman called for the list. One night a whole fire squad were blown to pieces at the top of the road. There were no corpses brought in, but their names were added to the casualty lists, one of whom was the brother of a friend of Betty's. The unclaimed corpses were wrapped in sacks and buried in a trench, an 'open grave'.

As the electricity was frequently cut off, the nurses had to carry out their duties by the light of hurricane lanterns. There was an emergency supply of electricity for the operating theatres. One morning there was no hot water in the hospital. Within minutes there was a procession of women in curlers and carpet slippers, ascending the hospital steps carrying kettles and saucepans of boiling water. On another occasion, hot water bottles were needed and in no time at all there was a pile three feet high.

Whenever the air-raid siren sounded, Mr Moore, the curate and Wally the warden would appear as if from nowhere. These two men inspired confidence in the staff and were a great standby. They would turn their hands to anything, whether it was carrying stretchers or washing dishes. On one occasion Mr Moore volunteered to remove an unexploded bomb. He was a tremendous source of spiritual strength. When he left to be an army chaplain he was greatly missed.

The ordinary patients had been evacuated to safer hospitals in the country, and St. Mary's had become a casualty clearing station. When there was a lull in the bombing they might be without any patients. A room in the basement of the half built outpatients' department was turned into a recreation room for the staff, who kept their spirits up with dancing, playing darts, or knitting and needlework. There was also a dormitory for the nurses and sleeping quarters for the medical staff.

Betty was asked to coach the students taking examinations. She had no ambition to be a tutor, she loved the patients too much. However, as there was a lull in the blitz and she felt she could help the students better if she had more knowledge, she arranged to take a part time course at Battersea Polytechnic three afternoons a week. This meant that after about three hours sleep in the morning, she had to get up and travel to Battersea by Underground to attend the 2 pm class. She was back in Plaistow by 5 pm and after a short rest, was on duty at 8 pm. It was the autumn term. After a few weeks, Miss Brinton, the principal of the department, offered her a scholarship for a full time crash course, which was being arranged because of wartime conditions.

The scholarship only covered tuition. A friend, Elsa Dodwell, loaned her money for living expenses and she took lodgings in Lavender Hill, Clapham, with a retired nurse, Miss Yateman who, although very kind, was strict and ran her house like a Nurses' Home.

Betty found the course and the other students very interesting and enjoyed the break from hospital life. After completing the course and becoming a Registered Nurse Tutor, she was advised that although she had been a Night Sister, she required Ward Sister's experience. She accepted a post as Sister in an acute medical ward in Halifax General Hospital, which she enjoyed very much. Yorkshire and Yorkshire people held great appeal for her. Also, it was before the days of antibiotics, and recovery depended on good nursing care.

Nadia was now working in Sheffield, so when Betty had some time off she would travel over the Pennines by bus to visit her sister.

During her time in Yorkshire there were no raids on London. One morning Betty received a letter from Miss Hutton, Sister Tutor-in-Charge of Charing Cross Nurses Training School, with whom Betty had made friends at Battersea. Miss Hutton informed her that they were opening a Preliminary Training School (their first), and she had already recommended Betty to Matron. So if she was interested in running the school, under her direction, would she travel down to London for an interview as soon as possible. Betty was very happy in her ward and reluctant to leave her patients, but it seemed too good a chance to miss.

Miss Cochran, the Matron, was old and massive in size. She had been Matron for thirty years and remembered Lord Lister and carbolic sprays in the theatre. When Betty saw her looking huge and terrifying behind her desk, she had an almost uncontrollable urge to run away.

Miss Cochran barked, "Sit down." Betty sat nervously on the edge of a chair. Miss Cochran then barked, "How old are you?" When Betty replied, she said, "Not a great age. Her next question was, "Do you like teaching?" Betty said, "I don't know, I have never taught."

Miss Cochran put her hands on her knees, sat back in her chair and roared with laughter. "Then we don't know if we will end up in Buckingham Palace or Bow Street," she said, and from that moment the tension broke and they were the best of friends. Betty owed a great deal to the help and guidance she received from Miss Cochran and Miss Hutton.

The Preliminary Training School was situated well away from the hospital, in Fitzjohns Avenue, Hampstead. It was the Jesuit Retreat House, which had been taken over by Charing Cross when their nurses' home had been commandeered by the WRNS. The house was run to perfection by Miss Nuttal, an ex-Barts gold medalist and retired hospital matron, a rather awesome person, very strict but kind, with a great sense of humour. She treated Betty as if she had not long left the nursery.

It was the time of the doodle bomb raids. When the sound of the enemy planes shut off there was a pause, during which everyone held their breath until the bomb fell. In some ways these raids were the most frightening of all and meant that lectures were frequently interrupted. During one raid, the Marie Curie Hospital at the bottom of the road was bombed, and for many months they were searching for buried radium with a geiger counter.

Because of the blackout, lectures were given in the mornings and evenings and the girls had the afternoons free. One day a week Matron, who in spite of her age had modern ideas, insisted that the students should be taken on an educational outing to a museum or some other place of interest. They were a happy, hard working crowd, and in spite of being terrified of teaching at first, Betty enjoyed the work.

She renewed her friendship with a Bulgarian brother and sister whom she had met before the war when they were on holiday in England, and because of the war, were unable to return home. Betty spent much of her free time in their maisonette in Kilburn, and accompanied them to Bush House where Kyril Mangoff and his sister Helen Mangova, broadcast to Bulgaria. Bush House was the centre of overseas broadcasting to the continent. After the war, they had the joy of knowing that their mother had listened to their broadcast and recognised their voices; but before they could return home the Iron Curtain fell and they adopted British nationality.

Due to a letter going astray, Betty met and made friends with a distant cousin, Sally, who lived at the top of Fitzjohns Avenue in a women's club, and was a reporter on the *Hampstead and Highgate Express*. She took Betty with her when she had to report on some play, and they sat through many raids together.

Then there was an open invitation to spend any free weekend in a beautiful Elizabethan cottage in the country on the border of Hertfordshire, called 'The Crump', so named because there were the remains of ancient British fortifications in the garden. The cottage belonged to Meum Stewart, who had spent a week as a Red Cross worker at St. Mary's Hospital, Plaistow. She was a charming person who, before she broke her ankle, had been one of the famous dancing troupe, 'Mr Cochran's Young Ladies'. She had also been one of Epstein's early models before he started his grotesque work. She owned a lovely head in green stone made by him.

Meum entertained many interesting literary friends including the playwright Clifford Bax, brother of the King's musician, Sir Arnold Bax. Clifford Bax wore a beard and looked like a reincarnation of Shakespeare. It was a great relief, after war torn London, to sit by firelight in the inglenook and listen to them talk in their beautiful cultured voices.

But Betty also had friends of more humble and homely background, including the poorest in the East End.

The war was a great time for making friends. One of her dearest friends was 'Auntie Eva', a gallant widow who lived at Wembley Park. Her husband and six children all died of tuberculosis. Betty was sleeping on her front room floor when a bomb dropped, shattering all her windows, and she helped her to evacuate to the country the next day.

It was one glorious sunny evening when Betty went with a friend to the West End to see a film, *The Desert Rats*, about the army in Egypt. When they came out of the cinema the hooters were sounding and everyone was going mad. It was V.E. night: Victory in Europe! They joined the general tide of people travelling along the Mall to Buckingham Palace, calling for the King and Queen. It was an unforgettable, joyous night and wonderful to be a part of that happy, frenzied crowd, as they stood and shouted outside the palace.

War still raged in the Far East, and Betty returned to St. Mary's, Plaistow, in the combined post of tutor and assistant matron, before V.J. night (Victory in Japan). It was about two o'clock in the morning and Betty was still in a housecoat, when the hooter declaring victory began to blow.

The rest of the staff were in bed asleep, but she quickly roused them. In no time they were all out in the street dancing and singing with the East Enders. Someone had dragged out a harmonium and they were all dancing the 'Hokey-Cokey' and 'Knees up Mother Brown'. Oh what a wonderful morning. What a wonderful day!

The East Enders had suffered so much with the bombing, sleeping for years in Underground stations and shelters. They had never lost their courage or sense of humour, and now victory was theirs and how they enjoyed it! There had never been such a night!

They were survivors!

20

ST. NEWLYN EAST

The Second World War ended in 1945. Claude Sara was very tired and beginning to feel his age. As well as all the extra work, there had been the heartbreak of trying to comfort bereaved wives and parents. It had been a joy to hear the church bells peal once more and join in the village victory celebrations, but he felt it was time a younger man took on the running of St. Dennis parish. So he applied to the bishop for a transfer and was offered the living of St. Newlyn East. It was sad to leave old and faithful friends behind, and he and Muriel were very much loved. One of his parishioners remarked, "They cared for our bodies as well as our souls."

Newlyn East was a very different kind of parish. The church and vicarage lay in the heart of a quiet country village surrounded by verdant farmland, and life went on at a more leisurely pace.

The church was large and beautiful, with easy access to the vicarage. A fig tree grew out of the church wall, and it was reputed that if anyone picked a leaf from the tree or damaged it in any way, they would die within a year. The villagers took this belief seriously and would quote foolhardy people on whom the curse had fallen.

The vicarage was large and rambling, less compact than St. Dennis rectory. It had eighteen rooms and a number of outhouses surrounding a stable yard at the back of the house. In the front of the house was a pretty walled garden; but there was a much larger garden on the other side of the lane.

The first great event in the new home was when, on the 21st

February 1946, Nadia Sara married Stanley Delbridge. It was a pretty wedding, conducted by the Bishop of Truro. The bride was given away by her father, and looked charming in a long white dress, made by herself, and wore the family wedding veil. Food and clothing were rationed. She made her own wedding cake and did most of the cooking herself for the pleasant family party that followed.

Stanley and Nadia had met before the war at the bishop's garden party. His father was vicar of Mithian, but although a Cornishman, had spent many years in America. Stanley was eighteen before they returned to Cornwall. He began to court Nadia straight away but the war came along. He joined the Royal Artillery and was sent to India and Burma. They corresponded throughout the years, but there was a long period of silence when Stanley was part of 'the forgotten army'. He was very sick with fever. He brought a flower-like engagement ring home with him from India, an opal (Nadia's birthstone) surrounded by rubies. The wedding was a dream come true after so much waiting and heartache.

There were three children of the marriage, Mary, Robert (Bobby), who died tragically at sixteen, in August like his Uncle Lewis. This was a great grief to the family and opened up old wounds. Stephen was born five years after his brother.

During this time, Betty Sara moved from St. Mary's Hospital to be Senior Tutor at St. Peter's Hospital, Chertsey. She became homesick and longed to be near her small niece and nephew. So she took the post of Deputy Matron at Redruth Hospital in 1950.

Soon after arriving at Redruth, Betty was invited to attend a biology class to be given by Dr Turk, at a W.E.A. weekend, to be held in a hotel in Porth, near Newquay. This proved to be a turning point in her life. There she met and made friends with Alan Flawn, who was a member of the history group.

Alan had been an officer in the R.A.F. regiment during the war, and had landed on the Normandy beaches on D2 Day. He had travelled throughout a devastated France, Belgium, Holland and Germany to Berlin, where he had been stationed for some months. After the war he had taken a teacher training course and was teaching at St. Just in Penwith.

They were married on 2nd June 1951. Because Alan was a Roman Catholic, their marriage took place at the R.C. church of

St. Ia at St. Ives. Claude gave her away, in spite of his disappointment that Betty was not married at his own church, St. Newlyn East. The reception was held at the Porthminster Hotel, looking over the sea to Godrevy lighthouse.

Alan asked her to use her proper name of Elizabeth, so Betty Sara became Elizabeth Flawn.

After the wedding they made their home in an old farmhouse that Alan had rented on the Zennor cliffs. Some months later, 'The Daughters of the Cross' at St. Michael's Hospital, Hayle, asked her to run their training school for nurses, and this she did for many happy years.

They had only one child, Miriam.

Claude and Muriel Sara were getting older. Muriel still enjoyed public speaking until one day, when she was due at a meeting, she had severe chest pains. Determined not to disappoint anyone, she travelled to and spoke at the meeting, in spite of her agony. On returning home she collapsed, a doctor was sent for and coronary thrombosis was diagnosed. Absolute rest in bed was the treatment in those days, and Muriel was nursed at home for many weeks before being transferred by ambulance in the deep snow, to St. Michael's Hospital. It was her wedding anniversary, and the family wondered if she would ever come home again. She made a good recovery but some years later she had a second attack, when she was nursed at home by her sister Mabel, home from Canada. After this she became a semi-invalid. Due to a fractured ankle some time before, arthritis had set in and she was walking on crutches.

Claude was suffering from frequent attacks of bronchitis, and in 1955 he decided it was time to retire. In the same year, Claude's remaining brother died. Edmund Sara was seventy-three years. He had been Rector of Ludlow and Assistant Bishop of Hereford for eighteen years.

An old lifelong friend, Gladys Ellis, told Claude and Muriel of a house next door to her in Hayle, for sale at an reasonable price. After much discussion, they decided to buy it and move to Hayle, which held so many memories and associations for them both.

21

ADIEU

Ansley Villa is a four bedroomed, listed house with spacious rooms and a walled garden. It was the first home that Claude and Muriel Sara had really owned, and it was a great joy to them.

They renewed many old friendships and took a great interest in local affairs. Claude spent many happy hours sun-bathing on the sandhills which he loved, while Muriel sat in the car, enjoyed the view and talking to passers-by.

Both their daughters had moved near to them with their families, and they enjoyed family parties.

Claude and Muriel attended St. Elwyn's church and became involved in church affairs. Claude was in great demand as a relief, and on many Sundays took services in churches in the area, when they were without a priest for any reason. When he was in his eighties, he drove fifteen miles in a severe snowstorm to take midnight mass on Christmas Eve, in a large, bitterly cold and almost deserted church.

Although Muriel was not able to move easily and had given up public speaking to a large extent, she enjoyed going to meetings and social occasions of all kinds.

Claude had been president of the Penzance Royal Geological Society for some time. Some years previously, he and Muriel had been chosen to represent the Society at one of the Buckingham Palace garden parties. They very much enjoyed going to the monthly meetings of the Society and the various excursions arranged by them. The Old Cornwall Society supplied another interest.

Muriel spent a good deal of her time writing articles for *The Cornishman*, *The Falmouth Packet*, and *The Cornish Review*. Another hobby was cutting out anything of interest from newspapers or magazines and putting them in scrapbooks.

Suddenly one evening, Muriel had a severe retinal haemorrhage and became totally blind. After some weeks her sight was partially restored, but very much impaired. In spite of this she remained cheerful and did not lose her zest for life. She remarked to a friend, "Now God has taken my physical sight, perhaps He will improve my spiritual sight."

On 26th February 1966, Muriel and Claude Sara celebrated their diamond wedding. It was a joyous occasion. They were surrounded by family and friends. The house was full of love, happiness and flowers. The usual telegram from the queen arrived. But the highlight of Muriel's day was when Claude whispered tenderly to her, "I love you, I have always loved you and always shall love you!"

During their latter years Claude had a slight stroke and it was considered that they should no longer live alone. Nadia and her family moved into Ansley Villa to be with them.

On 25th January 1969, Claude died at home from pneumonia, after only a weeks' illness. On the last day of his life, he came back to Muriel as a young lover. She sat by his bedside holding his hand, and when she left him for a few minutes to allow his daughters to change his bed, he got out of bed to look for her. He was helped back to bed and a few minutes later gave a deep sigh and his spirit left him. In the afternoon he had received 'Last Offices'.

His daughters laid him out in his white priestly robe, the alb, and placed a crucifix in his hands. When his little granddaughter Miriam begged to see him, she whispered, "Oh Mummy he looks like a saint." Later she crept in quietly on her own to say a prayer at his bedside.

The next day, Sunday, after Evensong, his body was received into the church, to remain there until his burial. There was a touching little service attended by a number of the congregation. The Requiem Mass, followed by a funeral service was attended by a large number of people. As a procession of clergy followed the coffin out of the church, they chanted 'The Nunc Dimittis, Lord now lettest Thou Thy servant depart in peace according to

Thy word'. He was buried in Phillack churchyard on the sand hills, by the sea which he loved.

Muriel felt very lonely without her beloved, but bravely showed a smiling face to the world. She was encouraged to write and have printed three small books about her memories; *Cornwall Remembered*, which went into three editions and was charmingly illustrated by her niece, Beth Berriman. Muriel was later interviewed by David Mudd and appeared on television. This was followed by *Russia Remembered*, and finally by *More About My Cornish Friends.* On the day of her death, she was planning a book about Trinidad, notes of which have been used in the chapter on Trinidad.

In May 1975, Muriel was staying with her daughter Betty while Nadia was on holiday. Betty had been living for some years with her family at Cranford, on Foundry Hill, Hayle. Muriel became much weaker. She said to Betty, "My time is near. I can feel Father waiting for me. Give everyone my love, but do not grieve for me. It will be wonderful to throw off this old garment."

When Nadia returned from holiday, Betty was due to take a month's Introductory Course for the St. Michael's nurses. Muriel was given a choice of a room in the hospital or returning to Ansley Villa with Nadia. She chose to return home. For the month her daughter was teaching, she was determined not to interrupt her work, and remained fairly well.

On the night that the course finished, 13th June 1975, Muriel died of a stroke. It was a month before her ninety-first birthday.

After her death, Muriel's face seemed to change and she looked Russian. Had she been Russian in a previous existence? Who knows? There was a Mona Lisa smile on her face as if she had discovered a secret.

Her handbag contained an envelope, in which was a thirty-two verse poem written by Claude in 1909, on the theme that if he died first, he would wait for her and together they would go to the throne of God.